T0208626

The End of Whitehall?

Patrick Diamond

The End of Whitehall?

Government by Permanent Campaign

palgrave
macmillan

Patrick Diamond
School of Politics and International Relations
Queen Mary University of London
London, UK

ISBN 978-3-319-96100-2   ISBN 978-3-319-96101-9   (eBook)
https://doi.org/10.1007/978-3-319-96101-9

Library of Congress Control Number: 2018950269

Cover illustration: Ruben Meines via the Noun Project

Printed on acid-free paper

This Palgrave Macmillan imprint is published by the registered company Springer Nature
Switzerland AG
The registered company address is: Gewerbestrasse 11, 6330 Cham, Switzerland

There is nothing a politician likes so little as to be well informed; it makes decision-making so complex and difficult.
John Maynard Keynes

CONTENTS

1 Introduction   1

2 Government by 'Permanent Campaign'   23

3 The Growth of Political Advisory Staff   31

4 The Personalisation of Appointments   57

5 A 'Promiscuously Partisan' Bureaucracy   71

6 Conclusion   77

Bibliography   93

Index   103

CHAPTER 1

Introduction

INTRODUCTION

This book's purpose is to analyse the most significant changes that have taken place in the Whitehall model since the Conservative-led Government's formation in 2010.[1] The developments of recent years originate in previous initiatives, particularly the novel ideas for reforming the state initiated by the Thatcher and Blair administrations. The core argument is the traditional Whitehall paradigm is being replaced by the 'New Political Governance' (NPG), an alternative model centred on political campaigning, ministerial advisers, personalised appointments, and a 'promiscuously partisan' governing machinery (Aucoin 2012). The civil service has gone beyond a 'tipping-point' or 'critical juncture'. The nature of the state bureaucracy in Britain is being altered fundamentally.[2]

---

[1] The arguments in this monograph draw on my recently published research paper in *Public Policy and Administration*: 'The Westminster System under the Cameron coalition: 'Promiscuous partisanship' or institutional resilience?' 7th November 2017.

[2] Throughout I refer to the *British* state bureaucracy well aware that since the advent of devolution in the late 1990s, there are separate civil service functions in Scotland, Wales and Northern Ireland. The book is focused on the UK-wide administrative tradition predominantly concentrated in Whitehall.

© The Author(s) 2019
P. Diamond, *The End of Whitehall?*,
https://doi.org/10.1007/978-3-319-96101-9_1

NEW POLITICAL GOVERNANCE AND THE END OF WHITEHALL?

The concept of NPG is derived from the work of the Canadian public administration scholar, Peter C. Aucoin. He foresaw a paradigmatic shift in governance and public management in the Anglophone states.[3] Their bureaucracies are experiencing growing conflict and discord: in this environment, 'the propensity for perceptions of politicisation to grow becomes almost unavoidable' (Grube 2015: 318). On the one hand, civil servants feel vulnerable to attack. Their influence and privileges are diminished by politicians unperturbed when officials become the target of vilification. The former Cabinet Secretary, Lord Butler, complained of, 'an unprecedented spate of recrimination against named civil servants, made worse by the fact that much of it has been through unattributable, backstairs briefings'.[4]

At the same time, Ministers are increasingly frustrated at the incompetence and 'accountability deficit' that allegedly characterises civil service performance. After merely a year as Prime Minister, David Cameron was, 'fighting something approaching an attritional civil war with what his advisers call 'the machine'.[5] The appetite for reform of the Whitehall machinery on the part of the political class grew stronger.

It was not always this way. In previous generations, British government was perceived to be both democratic and competent, uniquely combining qualities of 'efficiency' with 'effectiveness', the envy of politicians everywhere (King and Crewe 2013: xi). The first post-war Prime Minister, Clement Attlee (1956: 124), boasted the British civil service was, 'unequalled in all the world'. Yet over the last thirty years, the reputation of Britain's public administration has become increasingly tarnished (King and Crewe 2013: xi).

This introductory chapter outlines the book's conceptual framework, clarifies the intellectual terrain, and then maps the period in which the traditional civil service model has allegedly been eclipsed. The chapter begins by considering the institutional roots of the Whitehall 'paradigm'. The chapter then turns to the recent history of Whitehall reform through to the Conservative governments of David Cameron and Theresa May. Finally, the chapter considers the remorseless rise of NPG as the autonomy and independence of Whitehall's bureaucrats has been assailed.

---

[3] Aucoin was referring to the United Kingdom, Canada, New Zealand and Australia.

[4] https://publications.parliament.uk/pa/ld201314/ldhansrd/text/140116-0001.htm Accessed 6th February 2018.

[5] https://www.economist.com/blogs/blighty/2011/03/david_cameron_versus_civil_service Accessed 12th December 2017.

The argument throughout is the Whitehall model is being radically reshaped. The state bureaucracy in Britain is subject to 'permanent revolution'. Two key claims animate *The End of Whitehall*. The first is the Whitehall 'paradigm' is being eroded to the point where it is scarcely recognisable. Secondly, the destruction of the British tradition of public administration is detrimental. In Weber's terms, 'politics' is being allowed to encroach upon and weaken the values of 'administration'. Increasingly, partisanship prevails over the pursuit of the public interest. The 'deliberative space' for policy-making has been denuded at the expense of good government and the public service ethos.

The heyday of the Whitehall model in the decades after the Second World War is perceived to have been a 'golden era' for British government. In many ways, it was far from 'golden'. Professional bureaucrats saw citizens as passive subjects of the Crown. The gentleman in Whitehall apparently 'knew best'. Conceiving policy change as pulling the levers of the centralised state stymied the progress of economic and social reform. Yet the challenge to the Whitehall paradigm over the last thirty years scarcely gives grounds for confidence. Fundamental constitutional principles have been breached. The climate of 'hyper-innovation' led to waves of confusing managerial reforms. As a consequence, the UK state is more exposed than ever to the danger of egregious 'policy blunders'.

THE WHITEHALL MODEL

The Whitehall 'paradigm' is a structure of governance that emphasises the virtues of non-partisanship, neutrality, parliamentary accountability, bureaucratic permanence, and most importantly, mutual trust between politicians and civil servants (Page 2010). The 'model' was elaborated by Colin Campbell and Graham Wilson in their seminal book, *The End of Whitehall: Death of a Paradigm?* (1995). The Northcote-Trevelyan reforms of 1854 and the Haldane report published in the aftermath of the First World War decreed that Ministers and officials were mutually dependent. Politicians relied on civil servants to provide objective advice and uphold constitutional propriety; officials depended on Ministers to safeguard anonymity and protect the privileges of bureaucrats, maintaining the 'monopoly' of the civil service over policy advice. According to the Armstrong Memorandum, 'The Civil Service as such has no constitutional personality or responsibility separate from the duly constituted government of the day'.[6]

[6] http://www.civilservant.org.uk/library/1996_Armstrong_Memorandum.pdf Accessed 6th February 2018.

The Whitehall model is a rational 'Weberian' bureaucracy. Politicians and administrators rely on one another but are 'distinctly separated', performing contrasting roles inside government institutions; officials are, 'bound by [their] obedience to the power-holder', while politicians are confident civil servants will protect them in the struggle for power (Weber 2015: 156; Savoie 2008). As Campbell and Wilson (1995: 9) attest, 'To understand British executive politics, one needs to understand the world of the politician, the world of the bureaucrat, and the interaction between the two'.

In Weber's ideal-type bureaucracy, civil servants carry out the instructions of Ministers but as administrators—a separate breed from politicians: 'The honour of the civil servant is vested in his ability to execute conscientiously the order of superior authorities, exactly as if the orders agreed with his own conviction' (Weber 2014: 19). The Whitehall administrative tradition is thus characterised by a 'loyalty paradox'. Officials loyally serve the government of the day, but *not* the partisan interests of the governing party (O'Malley 2017: 404). The Whitehall model is part of the European 'Rechstaat' tradition of a non-political civil service faithfully serving Ministers (Guy-Peters et al. 2005: 1292). According to Lord Vanisttart, former Principal Private Secretary to the Prime Minister (cited in Hennessy 1989: 483): 'The soul of our service is the loyalty with which we execute ordained error'.

The mutually respectful relationship between politicians and civil servants was the 'governing marriage' that shaped the British state in the aftermath of the Second World War.[7] The 'golden age' of the British postwar consensus rested on harmony between politicians and bureaucrats, unified by confidence in the state's capacity to transform the economy and society.[8] 'Individual greed' and the doctrine of the limited state were replaced by the 'collective good' manifested in the welfare state capitalism forged by Keynes and Beveridge (Hennessy 1992: 44). Faith in the institutions of government was almost absolute. The Whitehall model was tied inextricably to the notion of 'club government'; public administration was the preserve of the closed, largely male elite inhabiting the 'Whitehall village' (Marquand 1988; Moran 2003; Bruce-Gardyne 1986). As the former Cabinet Secretary, Lord Butler, reflected, 'there was a greater feeling

---

[7] https://www.civilserviceworld.com/profile-peter-hennessy Accessed 15th December 2017.

[8] It is worth noting that a number of civil servants who were employed in the Attlee Government in 1945 such as Hugh Gaitskell, Douglas Jay and Harold Wilson subsequently became elected Members of Parliament and Government Ministers.

of solidarity and companionship between Ministers and civil servants'.[9] Even the 'outsiders' penetrating Whitehall were part of the club. The policy-making procedures of the state were dominated by a narrow 'epistemic community' who held shared assumptions about the responsibilities of government. Keynes' biographer, Robert Skidelsky charts, 'the increasing absorption of academics into government service' over the course of the twentieth century:

> The growing use of experts in government...reflected the greater complexity of governing in an urban, industrial society. The First World War opened up government to university academics...[who] never ceased to see themselves as an extended arm of the state. (Skidelsky 2013: 264)

The experts who served the machine came from the elite universities of Oxford, Cambridge and the London School of Economics (LSE), founded by Beatrice and Sidney Webb to fuse social science with Fabian socialism. By the mid-twentieth century, those who operated in the bureaucracy predominantly had shared educational backgrounds, reinforcing the bonds of reciprocal loyalty and trust.[10] Their world-views were complementary. The British state was saturated with 'Whig Imperialist' and 'Democratic Collectivist' assumptions; Burkean gradualism was combined with new-found faith in Fabian technocracy (Marquand 2008).

The British system of government was believed to be highly adaptive, evolving to embrace new challenges. 'Historical institutionalism', a core theoretical framework in political science, maintains that organisations make incremental adjustments over time accommodating both 'internal' and 'external' pressures; where change occurs, it is consistent with past choices and institutional legacies (Pierson 2004; Van den Berg 2016). Much of the academic literature maintains that reform in Whitehall fits within a pattern of gradual movement rather than a disruptive break with the past (Lowe 2011; Halligan 2010; Page 2010; Burnham and Pyper 2008; Bovaird and Russell 2007; Horton 2006).

Civil servants are inclined by temperament to downplay upheaval. Reforms are believed to be consistent with the traditional virtues of the British system. Politicians create confusion by overhauling public administration but pragmatic civil servants have an unrivalled capacity to 'muddle

---

[9] https://www.gresham.ac.uk/lectures-and-events/the-civil-service-and-the-constitution Accessed 19th December 2017.

[10] R. Skidelsky http://www.skidelskyr.com/site/article/the-british-tradition-of-administration/ Accessed 4 December 2017.

through'. Yet historical institutionalism inures us from grasping where major, far-reaching changes occur. Neither does historical institutionalism take ideas sufficiently seriously (Guy-Peters et al. 2005; Pierson and Skocpol 2002; Thelen 1999; Thelen and Steinmo 1992). As we shall see, ideas about administrative reform 'are embedded in the design of institutions' (Beland and Cox 2011: 8). Ideas do not drive institutional changes alone, but 'underpin and legitimate' the redefinition of civil servants as managers, the growth of managerial practices, and the rise of the 'post-bureaucratic state' (Clarke and Newman 1997: ix).

The End of Whitehall's contention is that the paradigm has been uprooted over the last thirty years—the last decade in particular. 'Mutuality' between Ministers and mandarins has broken down. As trust dissipates, the political climate grows receptive to radical administrative reform ideas. Whitehall experienced more change than at any point in the entire century before (Hennessy 2006; Seldon 2017). Governments attacked the professional autonomy and independence of the civil service, disregarding the constraints enforced by the Whitehall village's 'gentlemanly codes' (Marquand 2008; Leys 2006). The nature of the British civil service and the functioning of the state bureaucracy have been profoundly altered. Across the Anglosphere, 'the Weberian state may now be in decline due to the dominance of newer reform ideas'; such reforms 'blur the boundaries' between 'politics' and 'administration' (Huxley et al. 2016: 274; Savoie 2008).

These institutional changes have far-reaching consequences. Increasingly, civil servants are too cowed to 'speak truth to power' and are increasingly afraid to think for themselves. The political climate is defined by the 'greater ideological partisanship of the political parties', while there is, 'less time and space for reflection on, and consideration of, evidence' in policy-making.[11] The risk is governments commit more 'blunders'; 'policy fiascos' occur even more frequently (Crewe and King 2013; Richardson 2017; Richards and Smith 2016). Blunders happen where governments fail to achieve their objectives or where policies are carried out, but there are unintended consequences; the 'collateral damage' does more harm than good (Crewe and King 2013: 4). In subjecting the civil service to 'permanent revolution', Ministers have paradoxically undermined Whitehall's policy-making capabilities. Politicians are busily pursuing their agenda of reform and transformation, but neglect what is required to ensure a reliable supply of well-informed public policy advice. Worst of all, Ministers undermine the space for reflection about long-term policy-making in government.

[11] https://www.psa.ac.uk/insight-plus/making-better-use-evidence-government Accessed 18th January 2018.

The Recent History of Whitehall Reform

It is hard to pinpoint the exact moment of change. The breakdown of traditional models originates in the tumultuous 'crisis years' of the 1970s. John Hunt, then Cabinet Secretary, reflected that during the turbulent decade, governing became increasingly, 'cumbersome…difficult [and] a bit of a shambles' (cited in Seldon 2017: 47). Tony Benn's actions as a Minister were a precursor. Benn did not 'trust' his officials given they were servants of the Crown; he believed civil servants were wedded to post-war 'consensus politics', unwilling to consider 'radical' options; moreover, Benn drew on alternative advice from outside the Whitehall machine, urged on by his special advisers and a cadre of socialist economists.[12] That critique of Whitehall orthodoxy from the Left was matched by an assault on the bureaucratic machine from the New Right.

The Weberian model's decline amidst political hostility to bureaucracy reflected the growing influence of the New Right in Western democracies; officials were deemed inefficient and wasteful; the British Prime Minister after 1979, Margaret Thatcher, railed against the 'small-c' conservatism of the civil service and sought to 'deprivilege Whitehall'; the American President, Ronald Reagan, spoke of 'draining the swamp' in Washington DC; the civil service was attacked as a wasteful drain on hard-pressed taxpayers (Savoie 2010: 14–17). Officials were beholden to vested interests, blocking ministerial initiatives that threatened their privileges: 'Any plan for the future which the Minister might have hoped to see realised are strangled and pushed aside by official administrative business' (Jacoby cited in Qvortrup 2005).

Changes in the economic policy regime came thick and fast. The move towards lower personal and corporate taxation in the 1980s compelled the civil service to shift its focus, delivering 'more for less' through 'hyper-innovation' in the public sector.[13] The role of the state changed from managing nationalised industries and social security to service delivery and financial efficiency; the priorities of the centre impinged on 'street-level bureaucrats' working at the frontline (Straw 2004). The legacy of the 1980s and 1990s was 'constant reinvention' of policy and never-ending reorganisation of public services (Richardson 2017: 14).

[12] http://blogs.lse.ac.uk/politicsandpolicy/the-lessons-of-tony-benn-as-a-cabinet-minister-breaking-the-rules-and-paying-the-price/ Accessed 7th February 2018.
[13] https://www.gresham.ac.uk/lectures-and-events/the-civil-service-and-the-constitution Accessed 19th December 2017.

Over the next 30 years, 'hyper-innovation' meant constitutional conventions were undermined. Collective Cabinet responsibility and procedure were jettisoned. Not surprisingly, the civil service was demoralised and weakened. Rival actors challenged the bureaucratic 'monopoly' over policy advice. The career structure of mandarins was renegotiated. Thatcher's 'individualistic style' and reliance on a tiny cabal of 'hand-picked' advisers threatened Whitehall's meritocratic principle. The Thatcherite reforms of the 1980s unpicked the fabric of British government. The UK was a *State under Stress* (Foster and Plowden 1998). When policies failed, there was a frantic search for 'scapegoats'.[14] State capacity was diminished as British government was increasingly 'hollowed-out' (Matthews 2012). Peter Hennessy (1995) noted the relationship between civil servants and Ministers became increasingly fractious. When asked what it meant to be a Whitehall official, the former Cabinet Secretary, Sir Richard Wilson replied: 'It was a bit like carrying a grand piano upstairs while people tried to poke you in the eye'.[15]

Changes to the government machinery continued during the Blair premiership. Whitehall was swamped by special advisers, part of the New Labour campaign machine prior to the 1997 election. 'Sofa government',[16] an air of disrespect for civil servants, and the toxic culture of media 'spin' were feared to be endemic. One journalist wrote: 'Tony Blair began his period of office as a supporter for the Civil Service's 'Rolls-Royce' machine. He changed his mind when he experienced the system in practice'.[17] Yet Blair's Government:

> Failed to solve the problem because he realised the necessity of fundamental reform too late…prime ministerial micromanagement cannot solve governmental incapacity except temporarily, in a few areas, and at the cost of efforts elsewhere.[18]

[14] https://www.gresham.ac.uk/lectures-and-events/the-civil-service-and-the-constitution Accessed 19th December 2017.

[15] https://www.theguardian.com/politics/2002/apr/09/Whitehall.uk Accessed 19th December 2017.

[16] The term 'sofa government' referred to the growing tendency under the Blair governments for decisions to be taken informally by covert networks of Ministers and political advisers rather than through the formal proceedings of the Cabinet.

[17] http://www.telegraph.co.uk/news/politics/9339642/The-Civil-Service-reforms-are-too-little-too-late.html Accessed 14th December 2017.

[18] http://www.telegraph.co.uk/news/politics/9339642/The-Civil-Service-reforms-are-too-little-too-late.html Accessed 14th December 2017.

As a consequence of Labour's reforms, 'The old model of Cabinet government [was] as dead as a doornail' (Hennessy 1998: 12). The former official, Sir Michael Quinlan, wrote:

> [I]t is neither surprising nor illegitimate that a Prime Minister of Mr Blair's abilities, energy and self-confidence...should have chosen to operate in a more centralized way than almost any predecessor...what is, however, open to question, as we survey the scene disclosed by Hutton and Butler, [is] whether the changes—often, it seemed, reflecting a marked impatience with collective process—always rested upon sufficient understanding that existing patterns had not been developed without practical reason, and that departing from them might therefore have a downside that needed careful consideration beforehand.[19]

New Labour continued the assault on the non-partisan civil service (Aucoin 2012; Fleischer 2009). The former Prime Minister, Gordon Brown (2017: 226), wrote that political advisers, 'may have had no power to make decisions but in practice they became among Britain's most important decision-makers...much of what the Cabinet now does according to textbook constitutional theory is, in practice, done by these advisers acting as a kind of unelected Cabinet'. Labour's changes raised fundamental questions about the role of advisers; in particular, how to: 'protect public service professionalism and to set limits on the partisanship of public servants' (Mulgan 2007: 508).

According to Rodney Lowe (2011: 1), civil service reform was, 'the culmination of the long-frustrated administrative revolution promised by the 1968 Fulton report: the transmutation of senior officials from 'generalist' policy advisers into 'professional' managers'. Civil servants must be 'doers' rather than 'thinkers' (Peters and Savoie 1994: 420). Yet while Thatcher wanted the civil service to operate efficiently like the private sector, accountability structures and institutions remained 'essentially intact' (Savoie 2008: 81). After 1997 in contrast, there is evidence the civil service was radically undermined; power was amassed at the centre; policy initiatives were imposed on civil servants by Ministers; the emphasis on presentation through the dictates of the 'permanent campaign' took precedence over policy-making; a multiplicity of agencies meant lines of accountability were blurred; the culture of target-setting contradicted the emphasis on quasi-markets in public

[19] https://www.britac.ac.uk/sites/default/files/13-wilson.pdf Accessed 21st December 2017.

services breeding confusion. Blair's legacy in Whitehall was problematic, epitomised by the errors and ethical quandaries that characterised the run up to the Iraq war—the Labour Government's most controversial action.

After 2010, the political and constitutional relationships at the heart of the Whitehall paradigm came under unprecedented strain. A Conservative-led Government was elected with big ideas for the structural reform of the British state. Their plans had seismic implications for Whitehall. In the next decade, the model began to change irreversibly.

NPG Under Cameron and the Coalition

This book's aim is to address developments in the state bureaucracy focusing on the Cameron and early May premierships. Whitehall 'watchers' insist the relationship between officials and Ministers reached an 'all time low'; the constitutional authority and status of the Whitehall bureaucracy was gravely undermined.[20] This claim might strike readers as surprising. After all, coalition governments aren't usually associated with major upheavals in public administration and the machinery of the state. There is a plausible argument that the presence of the Coalition ought to have worked against major reforms. Aucoin (2012), for example, observed that 'checks and balances' in the permanent bureaucracy of New Zealand during the 1990s arose from multi-party government.

The first Cameron Administration rested on a coalition agreement. The majoritarian nature of the Westminster tradition, where power is concentrated in the majority party at the heart of the executive, was questioned (Lijphart 2012). The Liberal Democrats exercised a 'restraining effect' on Conservative Ministers (Goes 2015: 93). In coalition, power, 'is more dispersed and government policies arise from negotiations' (Gay et al. 2015: 119). The rules of the game that prevail in the Westminster model centred on executive dominance, majoritarian democracy, parliamentary sovereignty, and centralised territorial power were superseded (Lijphart 2012; Flinders 2010).

This situation meant the structural power of the Prime Minister and his advisers was qualified. Another party had Ministers in four or five departments, with a political base at the centre in the Cabinet Office. Robert Hazell (2012: 68) concludes, 'The Coalition required a revival of Cabinet Government' reinforcing the Whitehall model's stability. Moreover, the context in which the Coalition governed was one of 'fiscal crisis' following the 2008–2009 financial collapse. Comparative research indicates governing after a crisis entails, 'a strengthening of the social and professional status of civil servants' (Van der Meer et al. 2015: 1).

Yet none of these factors restrained the Cameron Government from attacking the Whitehall model. The Conservatives were, in practice, the predominant power. There was little perceptible coalition effect. There was no Deputy Prime Minister's Office rivalling Number Ten. Nick Clegg (2016) bemoaned the lack of institutional resources. Whitehall retained the majoritarian structure bequeathed by the Westminster model. Civil servants were accountable to departmental secretaries of state rather than Ministers from different parties; Jeremy Heywood, the Cabinet Secretary, sought to avoid separate 'power centres'.[21] Whether the Coalition strengthened the resilience of the non-partisan public service moderating the encroachment of NPG-style reforms is deeply questionable.

THE POST-BUREAUCRATIC STATE

As importantly, Cameron's Administration came to power with radical intentions in reshaping the institutional framework of British governance. The Conservatives promised to forge a 'Post-Bureaucratic State', part of their 'addiction' to reform ideas that reflected the New Right's ascendency in the advanced industrial democracies in the wake of the financial crisis. The public sector had allegedly grown too large and needed to be cut back, not only because of the post-2008 fiscal squeeze, but because governments were less competent at resolving problems from welfare 'dependency' to family breakdown (Hilton 2015). Francis Maude, the Cabinet Office Minister who conceived the Conservative party's programme, maintained the failings of the civil service epitomised the bankruptcy of statism and sought to impose, 'a set of reheated private sector nostrums'.[22]

In a speech to the *Reform* think-tank, Maude claimed: 'The era of big government has come to an end not just because the money has literally run out…but it is literally shown to have failed'.[23] Similarly, the Prime Minister's strategist, Steve Hilton, insisted the civil service ought to be cut by 90 per cent; he maintained policy work should be contracted out to

---

[21] Interview with Whitehall Think-Tank Director, 30th September 2016.

[22] Interview with a former departmental permanent secretary, 6th April 2018.

[23] http://www.civilserviceworld.com/articles/news/cabinet-office-minister-francis-maude-you-dont-need-be-mp-do-my-job Accessed 18th October 2016.

think-tanks and the private sector: 'One of his justifications is that we once ran an empire with only 4000 civil servants—so how can we justify a Civil Service of 434,000 today just to run Britain?'.[24]

The UK has no formal written constitution or 'civil law tradition'. The executive has, 'an unusual degree of control'; governing arrangements are *ad hoc*, shaped by waves of reform to a greater extent than continental European countries. There is an endemic culture of 'hyper-innovation' across the public sector (Downe et al. 2016: 173).[25] Since the 1980s, the UK has placed greater emphasis on administrative reform than other advanced economies (Huxley et al. 2016). NPM has been a 'remarkable revolution' in which the Westminster nations were, 'the most aggressive reformers' (Kettl 1997: 447).

The 2010 Conservative manifesto averred that under Labour, 'bureaucratic control has replaced democratic accountability', while, 'the hoarding of power by...unaccountable officials in Whitehall [had] damaged society by eroding trust' (Conservative party manifesto 2010: 73). The document listed a series of initiatives having much in common with NPM reforms, although there was less emphasis on performance management through targets[26]:

- The public sector target regime ought to be abolished in favour of departmental business plans.
- All data relating to government performance, including the cost of staff and operating costs, must be published making the state more transparent.
- Whitehall recruitment was to be 'opened up'.
- Public servants earning more than the Prime Minister required their salary to be signed off by the Treasury.
- 'Quangos' and non-departmental public bodies would be vastly reduced.
- Procurement would be centralised, reducing costs; digital technologies would make government more efficient (Conservative party 2010: 68–70).

[24] http://www.telegraph.co.uk/news/politics/9269823/The-Civil-Service-comes-under-fire-from-the-Coalition-but-bashing-the-bureaucrats-can-only-backfire.html Accessed 18th December 2017.

[25] http://www.bettergovernmentinitiative.co.uk/wp-content/uploads/2013/07/Civil-Service-final.pdf Accessed 18th December 2017.

[26] Interview with a departmental special adviser, 20th October 2016.

Cameron exclaimed, 'the old, top-down, big government approach has failed'. Ministers complained the civil service was slow-moving and dysfunctional; officials were unresponsive to political demands (Eichbaum and Shaw 2007: 454). Bureaucracy was now a dirty word. Maude argued public administration must be reformed according to 'rational choice design principles' (Eichbaum and Shaw 2007: 454). Civil servants should not be left to do their jobs. The non-partisan public administration ought to be subject to political control ensuring officials would not undermine ministerial initiatives (Gourgas 2016). The Whitehall machinery should be augmented by new experts and actors. Maude thus had a potent plan for radically overhauling the UK administrative state.

New Public Management and NPG

How far was the Conservative agenda merely NPM-revisited? NPM's main focus in the 1990s was altering state-society relations, overturning the traditional divide between the public and private sectors while allowing market forces to penetrate government (Hood 2007; Matthews 2012). NPM aimed to curb the traditional bureaucracy's power (Dunn and Miller 2007). Yet the Cameron Government's agenda was more akin to Aucoin's NPG. NPG has four characteristics:

- The 'integration of governance and campaigning'; its hallmark is the centralisation and concentration of power in the Prime Minister's Office.
- The growth of advisory staff relative to the permanent civil service; a growing inclination to undermine officials' 'monopoly' over policy advice.
- The 'personalisation' of civil service appointments.
- A government machine that is 'promiscuously partisan' (Aucoin 2012: 185–188).

Aucoin's concept of NPG and Donald Savoie's (2008: 16) notion of 'court government' are strikingly similar: power increasingly lies with the Prime Minister while, 'a small group of carefully selected courtiers' are appointed from outside the bureaucracy; there is a shift from 'formal' structures of decision-making to informal processes, particularly 'sofa government' where decisions are taken by close-knit teams of politicians and advisers. The policy-making process is driven by announcements and media management; the civil service is required to resolve presentational problems and justify decisions taken by Ministers (Savoie 2008: 16). The British system is more akin to 'court government' than at any time for a century.

Maude's agenda sought to re-impose political control over the government machinery. NPM aimed to leave managers 'free to manage'; in contrast, NPG wanted to discipline civil servants to follow political instructions. NPG focuses on intensifying partisan control over the central institutions of the state, denuding officials of influence while giving Ministers' power over policy-making. While NPM was intended to liberate governments from the burdens of bureaucratic inefficiency, the style of public management undermined the capacity of politicians to control the policy-making and implementation process (Matthews 2012; Skelcher 2000). After 2010, the non-partisan bureaucracy was increasingly conceived as a damaging obstacle to governance (Peters and Savoie 2012: 30).

Rather than encouraging fragmentation and 'hollowing-out', Maude believed governance reform ought to strengthen political influence. He imposed, 'new forms of hierarchical rule that sought to enhance the vertical co-ordination capacity in public governance processes' (Pedersen et al. 2011: 379). Maude aspired to politicise the policy-making process. This approach was centred on two 'interwoven tenets'; firstly, political representatives who 'make policy' should control public servants who 'implement' policy; secondly, ineffectual bureaucracies should be replaced by private sector management and 'quasi-markets' (Bakvis and Jarvis 2012: 12). While 'first wave' NPM accounts emphasised the importance of 'letting managers manage', subsequent versions stressed the importance of 'making managers manage' bolstered by competition and market forces (Kettl 1997: 449). In the Whitehall bureaucracy, civil servants should manage the policy process according to political imperatives.

In practice, NPG would only succeed if the structural power of bureaucrats was curtailed. In contrast to the mutual dependency foreseen by Haldane, Maude averred the relationship between Ministers and officials should be premised on 'principle-agent' theory. 'Principals' are politicians who give directions. 'Agents' are civil servants who put orders into effect (Le Grand 2006: 56). The influence of principal-agent theory on Maude's agenda was to reinforce the claim that bureaucracies have interests which contradict politicians (Niskanen 1971; Bakvis and Jarvis 2012). Weber warned that politicians would inevitably struggle to control an 'expert-dominated bureaucracy'; Ministers are 'dilettantes' or 'non-experts' in the affairs of departments (Savoie 2008; Weber 2015: 157). Ministers have to ensure bureaucracies bend to their political will. Principal-agent theory has its roots in the Chicago School and public choice economics (Van de Walle and

Hammerschmid 2011). The theory epitomises the dominance of the discipline of economics and its hold over fields such as public administration.

Maude's flagship 2012 Civil Service Reform Plan was a reaction against the previous generation of NPM reforms which in breaking up traditional hierarchies enlarged, 'The relative powers of bureaucracies and non-political actors'; managers not only gained autonomy but agencies were created outside Ministers' direct purview (Peters and Savoie 2012: 30). This made it easier for politicians to shield themselves from blame when fiascos occurred.[27] Yet as they competed in a tough electoral marketplace, NPM reforms made it harder for politicians to control the government machinery and operate according to the dictates of the permanent campaign.

While the Conservatives promised the end of the 'command and control' power-hoarding model, the Post-Bureaucratic State (PBS) aimed to enhance ministerial influence over the bureaucracy. Public administrators and policy managers had their feet held to the fire. Where civil servants were perceived to have failed or made egregious errors, they were replaced by think-tanks and management consultants from outside. Appointments would increasingly depend on politicians' preferences. Ministers confronted by a hostile media and sceptical citizens needed confidence in their inner circle.

The Conservatives' governance strategy was consistent with NPG. NPG overturned the fundamental premise of the Weberian model that 'politics' and 'administration' are separate domains with their own constitutional authority and legitimacy. Under NPG, the 'administrative' sphere is subsumed to the 'political' sphere. The distinction is then increasingly blurred. The institutions and norms conceived by Weber (2014: 12), 'the development of modern officialdom into a highly qualified, professional labour force, specialized in expertness through long years of preparatory training', were put at risk. The dictates of the 'permanent campaign' and the 'consumer-model of political choice' increasingly dominated the workings of government (Leys 2006). As one former Downing Street adviser acknowledged, 'In the British and American system, there is far too much power for people who are good at polls and very short-term politics'.[28] The 'winner-takes-all' culture of the British political system militates against the 'deliberative' evidence-based policy style (King and Crewe 2013: 390).

---

[27] That said, in the case of the Prisons' Agency and the Home Secretary, Michael Howard in the early 1990s, the Ministers attempt to escape blame for breaches of prison security did significant damage to his political career.

[28] Interview with former Head of the Number Ten Policy Unit, 17th February 2011.

THE STRUCTURE OF THE BOOK

This book provides an account of institutional change at a critical moment in UK politics. Whitehall is overseeing Britain's departure from the European Union (EU). Numerous issues are rising up the agenda from the demographic pressures of ageing to the impact of climate change. The programme of fiscal austerity is having a transformative effect. Across Whitehall, there has been a drastic reduction in the workforce; agencies have been restructured; the responsibilities of the bureaucracy have been renegotiated. Outside central government, public sector organisations are required to deliver 'more for less'; the size of the state has been cut back. We have moved beyond a 'critical juncture' in the state bureaucracy's development. Whitehall is markedly different to the governance model of fifty or one hundred years ago. Change is becoming irreversible.

In making this argument, the book is structured in the following way. There are four substantive chapters that consider how the Whitehall model has been replaced by NPG: government by 'permanent campaign'; the growth of advisory staff; the 'personalisation' of appointments; and the emergence of a 'promiscuously partisan' bureaucracy. The concluding chapter draws together the central themes. The volume builds on seven years of scholarly research, numerous discussions with actors in Whitehall, and a range of secondary documents including parliamentary and think-tank reports.[29] The aim is to make sense of key developments in Whitehall, contributing towards a substantive body of comparative scholarship on structural change in public administration and the core executive.

The recent literature on British government and the civil service has been dominated by historical institutionalism which exaggerates continuity and the influence of past legacies (Pierson 2004). To be sure, traditional hierarchies, norms and conventions persist. But they become increasingly anachronistic as the Whitehall machine is reshaped by NPG. Analysts have long warned that the Whitehall model is breaking down (Campbell and Wilson 1995; Page 2010; Aucoin 2012). The capacity of civil servants to fight back is becoming more constrained. Officials have suffered an alarming decline in status amid the erosion of trust:

[29] A series of semi-structured interviews were carried out from September 2016 to April 2018. A further seven interviews that inform this book were undertaken from 2011 to 2013. Interviewees consisted of former Cabinet Secretaries, three permanent secretaries, two former special advisers, and a variety of senior civil servants in Whitehall departments. The interviews were conducted under the Chatham House Rule. All of the sources are kept anonymous.

Heads of department [in the civil service] used to be regarded with some awe. They were people of weighty experience, wise and powerful, if deliberately remote and at least partially anonymous. They worked in the shadows, advising, managing and influencing the direction of their respective countries. They were the mandarins, recognised as the real rulers, the providers of continuity. Their reputation is now far more mixed. (Weller and Rhodes cited in Savoie 2008: 11)

Mutual dependency between civil servants and Ministers has collapsed. Ministers blame officials when major projects fail; Iain Duncan Smith slammed his Permanent Secretary at DWP, Robert Devereux, for being 'asleep at the wheel'; politicians believe civil servants are not being held to account for mistakes; there is a growth of 'off-the-record' briefing which has eroded goodwill in the 'governing marriage'.[30]

The capacity of officials to offer robust advice grounded in evidence is eroding with alarming consequences. In an interview after succeeding Cameron as Prime Minister, Theresa May was open about her frustrations; she implored of officials, 'Don't try to tell me what you think I want to hear. I want your advice. I want the options. Then politicians make the decisions' (cited in Forsyth and Nelson 2016). But civil servants have manifestly lost confidence. As Prime Minister, May continued the shake-up of the Whitehall machine, 'excluding junior Ministers and officials from much decision-making relying almost exclusively on her two advisers, Nick Timothy and Fiona Hill'.[31] Dissenters in the civil service were removed. Number Ten centralised power to an unprecedented degree. The axiom of the post-war settlement that the state and public servants are a force that promotes the public good has been demolished.

CONCLUSION

The End of Whitehall is not only about the institutional demise of the civil service, but an erosion of the idea that governments and public bureaucracies have the capacity to improve society. The decline in the reputation of Whitehall matters. The evidence indicates well governed societies are healthier, more prosperous, less violent and more cohesive (Runciman 2014). In his seminal treatise, *The Prince*, Niccolo Machiavelli claimed

---

[30] http://qmulcgl.blogspot.co.uk/2013/12/why-cant-ministers-and-senior-servants.html Accessed 6th February 2018.

[31] Quoted in http://www.civilservant.org.uk/index.html#reform Accessed 2nd February 2018.

efficient, competently managed states: 'are full of good institutions…conducive to the security of kind and the realm'. The aim of the PBS and NPG was to strengthen politicians' leverage in the policy-making process. Yet in seeking to enlarge the influence of 'politics' over 'administration', Ministers undermine their capacity to fulfil their promises, while markedly increasing their exposure to delivery 'fiascos'.

BIBLIOGRAPHY

Attlee, C. A. R. (1956). Civil Servants, Ministers, Parliament and the Public. In W. Robson (Ed.), *The Civil Service in Britain and France*. London: Steven & Sons.

Aucoin, P. (2012). New Political Governance in Westminster Systems: Impartial Public Administration and Management Performance at Risk. *Governance, 25*(2), 177–199.

Bakvis, H., & Jarvis, M. (Eds.). (2012). Introduction: Peter C. Aucoin: From New Public Management to New Political Governance. In *From New Public Management to New Political Governance*. McGill-Queens University Press.

Beland, D., & Cox, R. H. (2011). *Ideas and Politics in Social Science Research*. Oxford: Oxford University Press.

Bovaird, T., & Russell, K. (2007). Civil Service Reform in the UK 1999–2005: Revolutionary Failure or Evolutionary Success? *Public Administration, 85*(2), 301–328.

Brown, G. (2017). *My Life, Our Times*. London: Penguin Random House.

Bruce-Gardyne, J. (1986). *Inside the Whitehall Village: Ministers and Manadarins*. London: Sidgwick & Jackson.

Burnham, P., & Pyper, J. (2008). *Britain's Modernised Civil Service*. Basingstoke: Palgrave Macmillan.

Campbell, C., & Wilson, G. (1995). *The End of Whitehall? Death of a Paradigm*. Oxford: Blackwells.

Clarke, J., & Newman, J. (1997). *The Managerial State*. London: Sage.

Clegg, N. (2016). *Politics: Between the Extremes*. London: Bodley Head.

Conservative Party. (2010). *General Election Manifesto 2010: An Invitation to the People of Britain*. London: The Conservative Party.

Crewe, I., & King, A. (2013). *The Blunders of Our Governments*. London: One World Publications.

Downe, J., Andrews, R., & Guarneros-Meza, V. (2016). A Top-Down, Customer-Orientated Approach to Reform: Perceptions from UK Civil Servants. In G. Hammerschmid, S. Van de Walle, R. Andrews, & B. Bezes (Eds.), *Public Administration Reforms in Europe: The View from the Top*. Cheltenham: Edward Elgar Publishing.

Dunn, W. M., & Miller, D. Y. (2007). A Critique of the New Public Management and the Neo-Weberian State: Advancing a Critical Theory of Administrative Reform. *Public Organization Review, 7*(1), 345–358.

Eichbaum, C., & Shaw, R. (2007). Ministerial Advisers and the Politics of Policy-Making: Bureaucratic Permanence and Popular Control. *Australian Journal of Public Administration, 66*(4), 453–467.

Fleischer, J. (2009). Power Resources of Parliamentary Executives: Policy Advice in the UK and Germany. *West European Politics, 32*(1), 196–214.

Flinders, M. (2010). The New British Constitution. *Political Studies Review, 8*(2), 262–263.

Forsyth, J., & Nelson, F. (2016, December 10). Theresa May Interview: I Get so Frustrated with Whitehall. *The Spectator.*

Foster, C., & Plowden, W. (1998). *The State Under Stress.* Buckingham: Open University.

Gay, O., Schleiter, P., & Belu, V. (2015). The Coalition and the Decline of Majoritarianism in the UK. *Political Quarterly, 86*(1), 118–124.

Goes, E. (2015). *The Labour Party Under Ed Miliband.* Manchester: Manchester University Press.

Grube, D. (2015). Responsibility to Be Enthusiastic? Public Servants and the Public Face of 'Promiscuous Partisanship'. *Governance, 28*(3), 305–320.

Guy-Peters, B. G., King, D., & Pierre, J. (2005). The Politics of Path Dependency: Political Conflict in Historical Institutionalism. *The Journal of Politics, 67*(4), 1275–1300.

Halligan, J. (2010). The Fate of Administrative Tradition in Anglophone Countries During the Reform Era. In M. Painter & B. G. Guy-Peters (Eds.), *Tradition and Public Administration.* Basingstoke: Palgrave Macmillan.

Hazell, R. (2012). How the Coalition Works at the Centre. In R. Hazell & B. Yong (Eds.), *The Politics of Coalition: How the Conservative-Liberal Democrat Government Works.* Oxford: Hart Publishing.

Hennessy, P. (1989). *Whitehall.* London: Fontana Press.

Hennessy, P. (1992). *Never Again: Britain 1945–51.* London: Jonathan Cape.

Hennessy, P. (1995). *The Hidden Wiring: Unearthing the British Constitution.* London: Weidenfeld & Nicholson.

Hennessy, P. (1998). *The Prime Minister: The Office and Its Holders.* Basingstoke: Palgrave Macmillan.

Hennessy, P. (2006). *Having It So Good: Britain in the 1950s.* London: Penguin.

Hilton, S. (2015). *More Human: Designing a World Where People Come First.* London: Allen Lane.

Hood, C. (2007). What Happens When Transparency Meets Blame Avoidance. *Public Management Review, 9*(2), 191–210.

Horton, S. (2006). The Public Service Ethos in the British Civil Service: An Historical Institutionalist Perspective. *Public Policy and Administration, 21*(1), 32–48.

Huxley, K., Andrews, R., Hammerschmid, G., & Van de Walle, S. (2016). Public Administration Reforms and Outcomes Across Countries and Policy Areas. In G. Hammerschmid, S. Van de Walle, R. Andrews, & B. Bezes (Eds.), *Public Administration Reforms in Europe: The View from the Top*. Cheltenham: Edward Elgar Publishing.

Kettl, D. (1997). The Revolution in Global Public Management: Driving Themes, Missing Links. *Journal of Policy Analysis and Management, 16*(3), 446–462.

King, A., & Crewe, I. (2013). *The Blunders of Our Governments*. London: One World Publications.

Le Grand, J. (2006). *Of Knights and Knaves: Motivation, Agency and Public Policy*. Oxford: Oxford University Press.

Leys, C. (2006). The Cynical State. In *The Socialist Register*. London: Merlin Press.

Lijphart, A. (2012). *Patterns of Democracy*. New Haven: Yale University Press.

Lowe, R. (2011). *The Official History of the British Civil Service: Reforming the Civil Service Volume I: The Fulton Years 1966–81*. London: Routledge.

Marquand, D. (1988). *The Unprincipled Society*. London: Jonathan Cape.

Marquand, D. (2008). *Britain Since 1918: The Strange Career of British Democracy*. London: Weidenfeld & Nicholson.

Matthews, F. (2012). The Capacity to Co-ordinate: Whitehall, Governance and the Challenge of Climate Change. *Public Policy & Administration, 27*(2), 169–189.

Moran, M. (2003). *The Regulatory State*. Oxford: Oxford University Press.

Mulgan, R. (2007). Truth in Government and the Politicisation of Public Service Advice. *Public Administration, 85*(3), 569–586.

Niskanen, W. A. (1971). *Bureaucracy and Representative Government*. Chicago: Aldine-Atherton.

O'Malley, M. (2017). Temporary Partisans, Tagged Officers or Impartial Professionals: Moving Between Ministerial Offices and Departments. *Public Administration, 95*(1), 407–420.

Page, E. (2010). Has the Whitehall Model Survived? *International Journal of Administrative Sciences, 76*(3), 407–423.

Pedersen, A., Sehested, K., & Sorenson, E. (2011). Emerging Theoretical Understanding of Pluricentric Coordination in Public Governance. *The American Review of Public Administration, 41*(1), 372–395.

Peters, G.-P., & Savoie, D. (1994). Civil Service Reform: Misdiagnosing the Patient. *Public Administration Review, 54*(5), 418–425.

Peters, G.-P., & Savoie, D. (2012). In Search of Good Governance. In H. Bakvis & M. Jarvis (Eds.), *From New Public Management to New Political Governance* (pp. 29–45). McGill-Queens University Press.

Pierson, P. (2004). *Politics in Time*. Princeton: Princeton University Press.

Pierson, P., & Skocpol, T. (2002). Historical Institutionalism in Contemporary Political Science. In I. Katznelson & H. Milner (Eds.), *Political Science: The State of the Discipline* (pp. 445–488). New York: Norton.

Qvortrup, M. (2005). *Memorandum to the Select Committee on Public Administration – Written Evidence.* London: House of Commons.

Richards, D., & Smith, M. (2016). The Westminster Model and the 'Indivisibility of the Political and Economic Elite': A Convenient Myth Whose Time Is up? *Governance, 29*(4), 499–516.

Richardson, J. (2017). The Changing British Policy Style: From Governance to Government? *British Politics,* Forthcoming.

Runciman, D. (2014). *Politics: Ideas in Profile.* London: Profile Books.

Savoie, D. (2008). *Court Government and the Collapse of Accountability in Canada and the United Kingdom.* Toronto: University of Toronto Press.

Savoie, D. (2010). *Court Government and the Collapse of Accountability in the UK and Canada.* Toronto: Toronto University Press.

Seldon, A. (2017). *Blair Unbound.* London: Weidenfeld & Nicholson.

Skelcher, C. (2000). Changing Images of the State: Overloaded, Hollowed-Out, Congested. *Public Policy & Administration, 15*(3), 3–19.

Skidelsky, R. (2013). *Keynes: Economist, Philosopher, Statesman.* London: Penguin.

Straw, E. (2004). *The Dead Generalist: Reforming the Civil Service and Public Services.* London: Demos.

Thelen, K. (1999). Historical Institutionalism in Comparative Politics. *Annual Review of Political Science, 2,* 369–404.

Thelen, K., & Steinmo, S. (1992). Historical Institutionalism in Comparative Politics. In S. Steinmo, K. Thelen, & F. Longstreth (Eds.), *Structuring Politics: Historical Institutionalism in Comparative Analysis.* Cambridge: Cambridge University Press.

Van de Walle, S., & Hammerschmid, G. (2011). The Impact of the New Public Management: Challenges for Coordination and Cohesion in European Public Sectors. *Administrative Culture, 12*(2), 190–202.

Van den Berg, C. (2016). Dynamics in the Dutch Policy Advisory System: Externalisation, Politicisation and the Legacy of Pillarisation. *Policy Sciences, 50*(1), 63–84.

Van der Meer, F. M., Raadschelders, J., & Toonen, M. (2015). Introduction. In F. M. Van der Meer, J. Raadschelders, & M. Toonen (Eds.), *Civil Service Systems in the 21st Century.* Basingstoke: Palgrave Macmillan.

Weber, M. (2014). Politics as a Vocation: Originally a Speech at Munich University 1918. In T. Waters & D. Waters (Eds.), *Weber's Rationalism and Modern Society.* New York: Palgrave Macmillan.

Weber, M. (2015). *Weber's Rationalism and Modern Society.* Basingstoke: Palgrave Macmillan.

CHAPTER 2

Government by 'Permanent Campaign'

INTRODUCTION

This chapter's purpose is to examine how far Whitehall has been captured by the ethos of the 'permanent campaign'. The concept of the 'permanent campaign' is centred on the idea that the government machinery should be used to advance partisan objectives, entrenching the electoral dominance of the governing party. Civil servants not only work for the government of the day, they respond to the demands of the political party in power. Under NPG, partisan campaigning and public administration are effectively merged. The separation of 'politics' from 'administration' elaborated by Weber in *Politics as a Vocation* has been egregiously undermined in the British machinery of government. The constitutional independence and authority of the permanent civil service is subject to unprecedented attack.

GOVERNING FROM THE CENTRE

The hallmark of government by 'permanent campaign' is the centralisation of power in the Prime Minister's Office (Aucoin 2012). Every Prime Minister since Thatcher sought to strengthen their powerbase in Number Ten. Britain has had a 'prime ministerial' rather than a 'Cabinet' system since the 1960s (Mackintosh 1962). In the febrile environment of politics, partisan activity is not something that occurs exclusively at election-time. The Government secures a 'daily mandate' using the media as the instrument of persuasion. New Labour's purpose in government was to win

© The Author(s) 2019
P. Diamond, *The End of Whitehall?*,
https://doi.org/10.1007/978-3-319-96101-9_2

second term. David Cameron and George Osborne fought to win a parliamentary majority in 2015 by attacking the fiscal profligacy of the previous administration. The method of 'continuous partisan campaigning' contaminated the institutions of governance (Aucoin 2012; Bakvis and Jarvis 2012: 16). The appetite to control the message created an irresistible desire to govern from the centre (Bakvis and Jarvis 2012: 16).

The dynamic of the 'permanent campaign' leads the Prime Minister to build up their authority at the centre. They create units to pursue policy initiatives. The government's strategic communications are enhanced through tools such as the 'Number Ten Grid' that control announcements and the external activities of departments. The rules of the game in Whitehall change. The centre believes intervention is legitimate to control public expenditure, to drive efficiency, but most of all, to oversee political communications (Richardson 2017).

The shift in 'governing style' undermined Cabinet government and imperilled the non-partisan civil service. There was a remarkable centralisation of power in 10 Downing Street. As Prime Minister, Tony Blair saw himself as Chief Executive, with departments and Ministers as agents of Number Ten; the system of collective government through cabinet committees was anathema (Seldon 2017). Deliberative policy-making was judged slow and cumbersome. Cabinet government was weakened. Vital decisions were taken among a small cadre at the centre. A debate ensued about the rise of 'presidential' government, but the parallels were misleading. An American President faces constraints that do not afflict the British executive (Foley 1998; Page 2010). One official commented:

> In the long sweep of history, it doesn't make sense to say this is a long march to a more presidential system. There are some institutional and structural factors that weigh towards a more powerful and coherent centre, but they are crucially related to contingent factors that are about the external environment and the power of the Prime Minister themselves.[1]

Civil service non-partisanship was undermined by the view officials should help Ministers achieve their political objectives. Officials were increasingly aware they would be side-lined or replaced if they did not respond to ministerial directions. Civil servants were less willing to tell Ministers they are wrong or their preferred direction was likely to have unintended consequences and negative effects leading to 'policy blunders'.

[1] Interview with a former Head of the Downing Street Policy Unit, 6th March 2011.

The disaster of the Poll Tax occurred in the 1980s as, 'key officials became infected with their masters' zeal'; there were too few voices of dissent (Butler et al. 1994: 215).

The evidence that decision-making authority has been centralised to allow partisan 'permanent campaign' governance is compelling; Number Ten acquired structural power to enforce 'message control'. During Blair's tenure, all media interviews and speeches had to be cleared through the Prime Minister's Press Office; policy announcements were allocated time on the 'Number Ten grid' (Savoie 2008: 249). Under Cameron, centralisation largely continued.

WHITEHALL UNDER THE COALITION

When the Conservative Government came to office, the incoming Prime Minister initially criticised Labour's wielding of executive power. Cameron complained:

> Politicians, and the senior civil servants and advisers who work for them, instinctively hoard power because they think that's the way to get things done. Well we're going to have to kill that instinct…We need to end the culture of sofa government where unaccountable spin doctors in Number 10…toss around ideas and make up policies not to meet the national interest but to hit dividing lines or fit the news cycle. So we'll put limits on the number of political advisers. (Cited in IfG 2014: 13)

Another observer commented, 'Cameron came into office and it was very much a reaction against the Blair years. Special advisers had been media operators, duffing up civil servants. Cameron put a limit on the number'.[2] The Number Ten Delivery Unit was dismantled. The Policy Unit decreased in size; more civil servants were appointed to Downing Street posts. The Coalition committed Cameron to cutback Number Ten's institutional capacity making greater use of Cabinet committees. There was a reduction in the number of special advisers. Cameron imposed a limit of two per department, a change examined in the next chapter. As a consequence, by March 2011 there were a total of 73 staff employed in 10 Downing Street compared to 145 during the Blair years.[3] The heads of

---

[2] Interview with Whitehall Think-Tank research fellow, 12th December 2017.

[3] House of Lords, 'Written Question: Government Departments: Staff', 14 March 2012, col WA72   https://publications.parliament.uk/pa/ld201212/ldhansrd/text/120314w0001. atm#12031477001015.

policy and implementation, Paul Kirby and Kris Murrin, reported to Jeremy Heywood (D'Ancona 2014). Cameron created, 'a civil service-led policy unit'.[4]

It is claimed a more collegiate style of governance prevailed with an enhanced role for Cabinet committees: 'The imperatives and dynamics of Coalition made this a necessity' (Theakston 2015: 6). The Coalition entailed negotiation between parties making collegiate decision-making vital. The role of the Cabinet Office Economic and Domestic Secretariat (EDS) was enhanced. The Whitehall machine, 'reacted very quickly. [They] quite smartly created mechanisms to deal with the fact you had two parties operating'.[5] Number Ten's role was to provide 'light touch' co-ordination rather than enforcing the Prime Minister's will among departmental 'barons'. As one official remarked, 'Inevitably coalition has placed a greater reliance on using the Cabinet committees and machinery (cited in Hazell 2012: 54). The Cabinet met more frequently; Heywood, the most senior civil servant, attended meetings of the Prime Minister's 'quad' (comprising Cameron, George Osborne, Nick Clegg and Danny Alexander) (D'Ancona 2014).

THE PERMANENT CAMPAIGN AND THE WHITEHALL BUREAUCRACY

Despite these qualifications, under Cameron the influence of NPG and the 'permanent campaign' grew. There was growing concern with political presentation and strategy. Partisanship further altered the tasks carried out by civil servants. Policy work was less about objective analysis and appraisal of options. There was a renewed focus on devising elegant justifications for decisions politicians had already taken; this type of 'demand-led policy work' was less robust, undervaluing expertise (Savoie 2008; Hood 2007).

Moreover, the Government Information Service (GIS) expanded after 2010, while the nature of government communications changed. Civil servants were no longer impartial transmitters of information; their aim was to actively 'sell' the government's message. When Blair's party came to power, his team were bemused by the quality of the GIS; they set about 'modernising' the communications infrastructure. The civil service responded by upgrading capabilities and importing partisan methods into

---

[4] Interview with a former departmental permanent secretary, 6th April 2018.
[5] Interview with Whitehall Think-Tank Director, 30th September 2016.

the heart of government. Infamously, the 'campaign war room' and the 'strategic communications grid' appeared in the corridors of Whitehall. The platonic ideals of neutrality and probity were sacrificed.

Under Cameron, despite protestations about micro-management, the institutionalisation of policy and communications advice at the centre grew. By 2013, a revamped Policy and Implementation Unit was installed with a political head and mandate to intervene in departments. Cabinet Office guidance on Extended Ministerial Offices (EMOs) issued in November 2013 stated that one member of each EMO must report directly to the Downing Street Policy Unit, reinforcing the strategic dominance of the centre.[6] The upgraded Policy Unit gave the prime ministerial centre a 'brain' and 'delivery reach into departments'.[7]

Cameron and his Chancellor, George Osborne, were angered by the failure of the centre's 'early warning system' to alert them to Andrew Lansley's plans for the NHS which sought to transfer commissioning powers to local General Practitioners (GPs). The NHS Chief Executive, David Nicholson, described it as, 'a reorganisation so big you can see it from outer space'.[8] The plans were contentious and had to be watered down to gain the agreement of Cameron's Coalition partners (D'Ancona 2014). The Prime Minister was caught out, unable to resolve the issue politically. Steve Hilton complained:

> Very often you'll wake up in the morning and hear on the radio or the news or see something in the newspapers about something the government is doing. And you think, well, hang on a second—it's not just that we didn't know it was happening, but we don't even agree with it! The government can be doing things...and we don't agree with it? How can that be?[9]

Hilton claimed without a strong centre, the civil service would manipulate politicians to thwart change. As a consequence, the Prime Minister rebuilt capacity to intervene, as all premiers have done since the 1970s: 'The centre is usually slimmed down, and then the centre is built back up in the search for mechanisms to deliver the government's priorities'.[10] A

---

[6] http://www.civilservant.org.uk/index.html#reform Accessed 6th February 2018.

[7] Interview with a former Head of the Downing Street Policy Unit, 6th March 2011.

[8] https://www.telegraph.co.uk/news/nhs/10724504/David-Nicholson-the-man-who-believed-in-being-ruthless-with-the-NHS.html Accessed 12th March 2018.

[9] Cited in https://www.theguardian.com/politics/2013/jan/13/david-cameron-steve-hilton-criticised-policy Accessed 6th February 2018.

[10] Interview with Whitehall Think-Tank Director, 30th September 2016.

Minister in the New Labour era insisted: 'We were right to drive from the centre. Once the foot had come off the accelerator, the results just plateaued'.[11] Under May, the concentration of power in Number Ten continued with even greater zeal. The dictates of the 'permanent campaign' leave prime ministers with little choice but to centralise power.

CONCLUSION

Officials in Whitehall are now expected to use skills appropriate to the 'political world' rather than the 'administrative world', blurring the distinction between 'politics' and 'administration' delineated by Weber (Savoie 2008: 229; Weber 2015). It is striking that the UK Statistics Authority recently upheld complaints against departments for the misuse of data. The former Secretary of State for Work and Pensions, Iain Duncan Smith, was reprimanded for making claims about the 'benefits cap' that were not supported by official statistics.[12]

These misdeeds indicate an invidious trend towards the debasement of the government information machine. The dictates of the 'permanent campaign' became more influential after the Cameron Administration took office. The centralisation of power in Number Ten and the installation of a large-scale media operation to further the governing party's partisan objectives have shown no sign of abating under May's premiership. The influence of political advisers has grown too, a key development examined in the next chapter.

BIBLIOGRAPHY

Aucoin, P. (2012). New Political Governance in Westminster Systems: Impartial Public Administration and Management Performance at Risk. *Governance*, 25(2), 177–199.

Bakvis, H., & Jarvis, M. (Eds.). (2012). Introduction: Peter C. Aucoin: From New Public Management to New Political Governance. In *From New Public Management to New Political Governance*. McGill-Queens University Press.

Butler, D., et al. (1994). *Failure in British Government: The Politics of the Poll Tax*. Oxford: Oxford University Press.

[11] Interview with former Secretary of State, 11th February 2011.

[12] https://gss.civilservice.gov.uk/contact-us/uk-statistics-authority/ Accessed 15th December 2017. https://www.theguardian.com/politics/2013/may/09/iain-duncan-smith-benefits-cap-statistics Accessed 15th December 2017.

D'Ancona, M. (2014). *In It Together: The Inside Story of a Coalition Government.* London: Viking.

Foley, M. (1998). *The British Presidency.* Manchester: Manchester University Press.

Hazell, R. (2012). How the Coalition Works at the Centre. In R. Hazell & B. Yong (Eds.), *The Politics of Coalition: How the Conservative-Liberal Democrat Government Works.* Oxford: Hart Publishing.

Hood, C. (2007). What Happens When Transparency Meets Blame Avoidance. *Public Management Review, 9*(2), 191–210.

Institute for Government (IfG). (2014). *Centre Forward: Effective Support for the Prime Minister at the Centre of Government.* London: IfG.

Mackintosh, J. (1962). *The British Cabinet.* London: Stevens & Sons.

Page, E. (2010). Has the Whitehall Model Survived? *International Journal of Administrative Sciences, 76*(3), 407–423.

Richardson, J. (2017). The Changing British Policy Style: From Governance to Government? *British Politics,* Forthcoming.

Savoie, D. (2008). *Court Government and the Collapse of Accountability in Canada and the United Kingdom.* Toronto: University of Toronto Press.

Seldon, A. (2017). *Blair Unbound.* London: Weidenfeld & Nicholson.

Theakston, K. (2015). David Cameron as Prime Minister. *British Politics Review, 10*(2), 6–7.

Weber, M. (2015). *Weber's Rationalism and Modern Society.* Basingstoke: Palgrave Macmillan.

CHAPTER 3

The Growth of Political Advisory Staff

INTRODUCTION

Over the last three decades, there has been a dramatic expansion of political advisory staff in UK government. The growing influence of political appointees has been examined at length in the media, as well as the academic literature on British governance. The television satire, *The Thick of It*, focuses on the role of special advisers in British government in contrast to *Yes, Minister*, a programme made thirty years previously, which cast senior civil servants as wily manipulators of Ministers. This chapter will examine the causes and consequences of recruiting an increasing number of political staff from outside the permanent civil service. The evidence is 'politicisation' has grown in recent decades as a consequence of the influx of appointees. The threat posed to the traditional Whitehall model from the escalation of partisanship is significant, upending the once sacred civil service 'monopoly' over policy advice.

The debate is nevertheless more nuanced than depicted by images of shadowy special advisers. The nature of the policy process has changed radically over the last thirty years. The growth of policy-relevant research, the impact of new technology, and the demand for 'user-driven' public services led Ministers to seek varieties of specialist advice from outside the permanent bureaucracy. Politicisation ought not to be confused with the legitimate search for expertise.

© The Author(s) 2019
P. Diamond, *The End of Whitehall?*,
https://doi.org/10.1007/978-3-319-96101-9_3

THE GROWTH OF SPECIAL ADVISERS

'Politicisation' is an ambiguous concept. Since the 1990s, 'there has been a growing tendency to employ politically appointed special advisers to service ministers' (Qvortrup 2005). Advisers epitomise Weber's emphasis on 'professionalisation'. Ministers bring apparatchiks with specialist training into government to assist in the battle for power. Harold Wilson was the first Prime Minister to appoint special advisers, dealing with, 'the burden of modern government…the immense volume of papers, the exhausting succession of departmental committees, of Party gatherings and meetings with outside interests'.[1] The Cabinet Office *Code of Conduct for Special Advisers* states they should provide, 'a political dimension to the advice and assistance available to Ministers while reinforcing the political impartiality of the permanent Civil Service by distinguishing the source of political advice and support'.[2] Officials claim to welcome the appointment of competent advisers:

> Permanent Secretaries/Director-Generals report they highly value Special Political Advisers (SPADs) as a working relationship has evolved whereby SPADs facilitate and position key messages from Civil Servants to be positively received by Ministers.[3]

Ministerial advisers are the alternative to politicising civil service appointments (O'Malley 2017: 409; Craft 2013). Their purpose is to ensure Ministers are not isolated in departments, and they pursue the government's political objectives (Yong and Hazell 2014). The Cabinet Office code states: 'In order to provide effective assistance to Ministers, special advisers should work closely with the ministerial team and with permanent civil servants, and establish relationships of confidence and trust'.[4] Ministers, officials and appointees are expected to work together in a mutually beneficial relationship to further the aims of good government.[5]

---

[1] Prime Minister Harold Wilson cited in https://www.ucl.ac.uk/constitution-unit/publications/tabs/unit-publications/158 Accessed 18th January 2018.

[2] Cited in https://www.ucl.ac.uk/constitution-unit/publications/tabs/unit-publications/158 Accessed 18th January 2018.

[3] Cited in https://publications.parliament.uk/pa/cm201617/cmselect/cmpubadm/253/253.pdf Accessed 2nd February 2018.

[4] https://www.google.com/?client=safari&channel=ipad_bm Accessed 22nd February 2018.

[5] https://www.google.co.uk/?client=safari&channel=ipad_bm&gws_rd=cr&dcr=0&ei=V26WWp7MA8mdsAeX3r3ACg Accessed 21st February 2018.

Political appointments have transformed the culture of British government. Advisers can be more influential in departmental policy-making than senior civil servants (Grube 2015). As one 'Whitehall watcher' observes, 'Special advisers made a huge difference by challenging the monopoly over policy analysis, acting as policy entrepreneurs in government'.[6] Political staff are a 'critical mass' within the government machinery that marginalise the civil service; the non-partisan bureaucracy is viewed warily as, 'an obstacle to be overcome' (Bakvis and Jarvis 2012: 16; Grube 2015). Secretaries of state have political support from junior Ministers; departmental boards with non-executive directors; Parliamentary Private Secretaries who 'link' Ministers to the party; politically appointed; and experts with specialist knowledge in a relevant sector.[7] Politicians thus have a vast 'entourage' at their disposal. The danger is political appointees prevent specialist civil service advice from reaching Ministers (Van den Berg 2016: 65).

There are approximately 120 Ministers and aides alongside 100 advisers challenging the policy-making elite at the top of the civil service.[8] A 'critical mass' of advisers allows the incumbent government to engage in a 'permanent campaign' and dominate the electoral marketplace. Not only have the number of advisers grown. The remit of advisers has widened from 'light-touch' political management to intervening in policy-making and implementation. For instance, Tony Blair's Policy Chief, Andrew Adonis, and Dominic Cummings, Special Adviser to Michael Gove in the Department of Education, were both directly involved in the procurement process for academy schools. Iain Duncan Smith's advisers devised the 'universal credit' policy almost single-handedly.

The Marginalisation of the Civil Service

As a consequence, bureaucrats are side-lined in the policy process, 'passive functionaries' confined to operational roles fulfilling the instructions of Ministers. The civil service undertakes three key constitutional and policy-making roles that are imperilled if officials are marginalised: maintaining 'safeguards' to uphold ethical proprieties and ensure governments act within the scope of the law; providing rigorous, evidence-based advice;

[6] Interview with Whitehall Think-Tank Director, 30th September 2016.
[7] http://www.bettergovernmentinitiative.co.uk/wp-content/uploads/2013/07/Civil-Service-final.pdf Accessed 6th February 2018.
[8] http://www.civilservant.org.uk/spads-history_and_comment.html   Accessed   2nd February 2018.

and offering an objective view, not telling Ministers, 'what it is they think the Minister wants to hear'.[9]

Although they rarely outnumber the permanent civil service, advisers occupy crucial positions of strategic influence through which they ostracise officials posing a threat. The machinery of government is used to conduct a 'permanent campaign' of electoral partisanship. The Whitehall historian, Peter Hennessy, insists special advisers:

> Create a weather system that reinforces the worst tendencies of the political class: an obsession with who is out to get them, both in the opposition and in their own party. I love the political class: they're indispensable. But they have their own little ways, and if the special advisers encourage still more of those little ways, we're in real trouble.[10]

Political advisers have the potential to be, 'destructive and damaging'.[11] The case of Jeremy Hunt's adviser at the Department of Culture, Media and Sport (DCMS), Adam Smith, is notable. Smith is believed to have become close to lobbyists employed by Rupert Murdoch to influence the Coalition Government's decision on *News International's* acquisition of *BSkyB* in 2011. The case raised concerns about misconduct and impropriety among political appointees. Smith acted without approval from the Secretary of State and DCMS Permanent Secretary. It was inappropriate for the special adviser to become involved in a 'quasi-judicial' process overseen by the department.[12] It is still unusual that advisers resign but not the Minister. Hunt was accused of failing to take responsibility for actions carried out in his name.

Politicisation is defined as, 'the substitution of political criteria for merit-based criteria in the selection, retention, promotion, rewards, and disciplining of members of the public service' (Guy Peters and Pierre 2004: 2). Several forms of politicisation undermine the Whitehall model. In 'partisan politicisation', an individual is appointed with a long-standing party affiliation; in 'policy-related politicisation', an adviser is recruited committed to policies favoured by the administration; in 'managerial

---

[9] http://www.bettergovernmentinitiative.co.uk/wp-content/uploads/2013/07/Civil-Service-final.pdf Accessed 8th February 2018.

[10] https://www.civilserviceworld.com/profile-peter-hennessy Accessed 15th December 2017.

[11] Interview with a former departmental permanent secretary, 6th April 2018.

[12] https://www.google.co.uk/?client=safari&channel=ipad_bm&gws_rd=cr&dcr=0&ei=Bn2WWvONBIPTkgWbnYmoCQ Accessed 20th February 2018.

Table 3.1 Special adviser numbers 2010–2017

	Total number of special advisers in Whitehall	Total number of special advisers in No.10 (PM and DPM)
2010	79	33
2011	79	33
2012	79	33
2013	94	40
2014	103	40
2015	89	32
2016	86	32
2017	88	32

Source: https://www.gov.uk/government/publications/special-adviser-data-releases-numbers-and-costs Accessed 21st October 2015 Accessed 18th December 2017

politicisation', officials are replaced when a change of government occurs (Qvortrup 2005). As Qvortrup attests, policy-related and managerial politicisation are as important as the dramatic influx of advisers into Whitehall.

Table 3.1 demonstrates the number of special advisers grew in the Cameron years, reaching a peak of 107 in 2014 (Haddon 2016). More advisers have been in Number Ten under the Conservatives than under Tony Blair or Gordon Brown.[13] In 2012, the Downing Street Policy and Implementation Unit was expanded. The Unit was modelled on the Prime Minister's Delivery Unit (PMDU) designed by Michael Barber during the Blair premiership (Haddon 2016). A political head, Jo Johnson MP, was appointed to develop ideas for the 2015 manifesto. The Policy Unit pursued the Prime Minister's personal agenda whereas the Cabinet Office merely ensured government functioned effectively (Peters and Savoie 1994: 420). The Government then rewrote the Special Advisers' Code, allowing advisers, 'to convey to officials Ministers' views, instructions and priorities'.[14] Between 1997 and 2013, there were 26 examples of political appointees allegedly acting inappropriately and breaching the Code.[15]

[13] https://www.democraticaudit.com/2018/01/23/just-how-special-are-special-advisers-within-the-uk-civil-service/ Accessed 18th December 2018.
[14] Cited in http://www.civilservant.org.uk/spads-history_and_comment.html Accessed 22nd January 2018.
[15] http://www.civilservant.org.uk/library/2013_SpAds_and_Misconduct.pdf Accessed 5th February 2018.

EXTENDED MINISTERIAL OFFICES

While the academic literature (Blick 2004; Rhodes 2011a; Gains and Stoker 2011) and popular television programmes focus on special advisers, the informal growth of appointees in private offices with a background sympathetic to the Minister poses the greatest threat to the Whitehall model. There are few specific regulations governing such appointments. The back and forth of employees from think-tanks and NGOs into central government has rarely been examined. The growth of 'policy-related politicisation' where officials sympathetic to government policy are appointed has been marked. A leading expert avers in the case of 'irregular appointees', 'It is too early to tell whether it is a direction of travel or a blip'.[16] The evidence is: 'The informal cap on [special adviser] numbers has...been circumvented by appointing individuals as time-limited civil servants' (cited in Richardson 2017: 15).

The 2012 Civil Service Reform Plan and IPPR report on civil service accountability recommended Extended Ministerial Offices (EMOs). EMOs enable Ministers to bring personal appointees into Whitehall. The Prime Minister justified EMOs on the grounds they provide, 'some experts, a bit of implementation, some special advisers. That's quite like what the Prime Minister has. It's quite like what some Ministers have already put in place. I think it's growing organically. I'm helping giving it a nudge along'.[17]

Although the take-up of EMOs was limited and permanent secretaries had the power to veto them, ministerial offices were part of a trend in which sympathetic appointees are brought into government (Gouglas and Brans 2016). Hennessy noted the Civil Service Commission charged with upholding Northcote-Trevelyan was concerned about EMOs: 'To abandon the Northcote-Trevelyan principles would be a national own goal of considerable proportions'.[18] Giving evidence to the Public Administration Select Committee (PASC), Hennessy cautioned against 'seeping politicisation'.[19] The *Better Government Initiative* warned ministerial

---

[16] Interview with Whitehall Think-Tank research fellow, 12th December 2017.

[17] https://publications.parliament.uk/pa/ld201314/ldhansrd/text/140116-0001.htm Accessed 6th February 2018.

[18] https://publications.parliament.uk/pa/ld201314/ldhansrd/text/140116-0001.htm Accessed 6th February 2018.

[19] http://www.publications.parliament.uk/pa/cm201213/cmselect/cmpubadm/c644-i/c644i.pdf.

offices, 'risk becoming institutionalised cocoons impervious to dissenting opinions or unwelcome facts'.[20] 'Because the relationship was [now] so bad', officials saw EMOs, 'as another way of pushing them to the back of the queue'.[21]

There was concern EMOs would shield Ministers from unwelcome advice. In the Australian system, Minister's offices are physically separate from the permanent bureaucracy; as a consequence, 'The non-partisan public service has virtually no place within Ministers' offices (O'Malley 2017: 410). In Whitehall, there were more 'irregular' appointments while the status of officials was undermined by the incipient influx of think-tanks and management consultancies.

Challenging the Civil Service 'Monopoly' over Policy Advice

As a consequence, the civil service 'monopoly' over policy advice has fallen apart; officials have ceased to be, 'primary policy-makers'.[22] The system has been mutating since the Second World War; there was a recognition Whitehall had to become more receptive to outside advice. In British government, observers claim:

> There has never been a period where the civil service had a monopoly of policy in Britain, absolutely never. Even in the highpoint of very assertive cabinet secretaries and a central civil service, you had an endless stream of many academics going in and out of government. You had strong research departments in the parties, you had whole networks and sources flowing into policy from think-tanks…I don't buy this story that there was a monopoly and then it was broken open by special advisers and think-tanks.[23]

Government where anonymous civil servants have the monopoly over policy formation long since ceased (Wildavsky 1979). The closed world of Whitehall is finished. The civil service can still work with Ministers to develop policies, but approaches are changing as a result of new technolo-

[20] http://www.bettergovernmentinitiative.co.uk/wp-content/uploads/2013/07/Civil-Service-final.pdf Accessed 18th December 2017.

[21] Interview with a former departmental permanent secretary, 6th April 2018.

[22] Interview with a former departmental permanent secretary, 6th April 2018.

[23] Interview with former Head of the Cabinet Office Strategy Unit (PMSU), February 2012.

gies, the growth of policy-relevant research, the emergence of more sophisticated forms of evidence, and the rise of a diverse citizenry with different expectations of government.[24] It is no longer justifiable for policy problems to be defined in a narrow space jealously guarded by bureaucrats, nor can civil servants be 'tone deaf' to politics; they need to be conscious when 'policy windows' are opening up; they must balance politicians' thirst for rapid solutions with the tradition of evidence-led deliberation.[25] Yet as one Permanent Secretary points out, despite the pluralised structure of policy-making, civil servants still control the submissions Ministers receive, as they did in the 1960s and 1970s:

> Policy officials are always desperate for new ideas, new insights, new evidence: the key thing is that their advice has to be read by ministers. Advisers cannot rewrite or censor policy submissions. Submissions go direct to the Minister.[26]

Despite Freedom of Information legislation, the conventions of secrecy remain broadly intact; confidential advice to Ministers is not disclosed; senior civil servants perceive themselves to be 'policy-makers' not operational or delivery staff, just as they did fifty years ago (Haddon 2016; Rhodes 2011b). The anonymity of officials is defensible on the grounds civil servants cannot respond to public criticism. Confidentiality is necessary for officials to speak fearlessly. Civil servants are sanguine about outside policy actors, claiming:

> Think-tanks tend to over-estimate their importance; they rarely produce genuinely new ideas. Also they cannot produce detailed or really rigorous thinking about policy. Most new thinking is actually internally generated in the civil service.[27]

As such, 'the [civil service] monopoly has ended but one shouldn't go to the opposite extreme and say civil servants don't matter'.[28] As one observer points out:

---

[24] https://www.google.co.uk/?client=safari&channel=ipad_bm&gws_rd=cr&dcr=0&ei=xFiqWr2OLoifgAahh4iwDA Accessed 11th March 2018.

[25] https://www.google.co.uk/?client=safari&channel=ipad_bm&gws_rd=cr&dcr=0&ei=xFiqWr2OLoifgAahh4iwDA Accessed 12th March 2018.

[26] Interview with a departmental permanent secretary, 19th October 2016.

[27] Interview with a departmental permanent secretary, 19th October 2016.

[28] Interview with a departmental permanent secretary, 19th October 2016.

Civil servants can still control the advice ministers see. I remember seeing Steve Hilton in action…his party piece was about how few Whitehall policy submissions were about new initiatives. But…you still have to run what you're doing…people still have to have their pensions paid, you have floods. The premium on the civil service is a classic one…you've got to run the existing system. The public attention is on change, but the premium on the civil service is keeping the system running…people need passports and pensions and a health service.[29]

The focus on policy reinvention neglects the need to maintain the existing bureaucratic machinery, the function chiefly fulfilled by the civil service.

OPENING UP THE MARKETPLACE OF IDEAS

Yet time and again under Cameron, the policy role of officials was attacked. The 'policy advising capacity' of the civil service was diminished (Van den Berg 2016). In the UK, the role of the civil service was systematically undermined,[30] paving the way for opening up the marketplace of ideas. Civil servants were believed to be too 'insular' and 'closed', unwilling to work with external stakeholders; there was a gap between those who design policy and those who implement policy, reinforced by lack of frontline knowledge and detachment from 'street-level bureaucrats'; officials were thought to be weak at understanding innovation, including the importance of policy evaluation; there was insufficient clarity about the role of the civil service in policy-making.[31] The fundamental problem from the New Right's perspective was officials are, 'monopoly suppliers of their service' (Niskanen 1994: 271).

After 2010, there was evidence of profound dissatisfaction with the civil service. Many politicians maintain the bureaucracy's performance was inadequate. One insider remarked Maude, 'was appalled by the state of the civil service. Nothing really worked properly in government. Too much

---

[29] Interview with former Head of a Whitehall think-tank, 30th September 2016.

[30] Thomas Balogh's famous essay published in 1959, 'The Apotheosis of the Dilettante', set the tone several decades ago by claiming that civil servants in Britain had been educated in such a way as to develop, 'a purposefully useless, somewhat dilettante erudition, which would keep dangerous thoughts well away' (Balogh 1959: 112).

[31] https://www.ippr.org/publications/innovations-in-governmentinternational-perspectives-on-civil-service-reform Accessed 11th March 2018.

policy was ill thought through'.[32] Angered by the influence of the civil service and its capacity to thwart change, Michael Gove published an article in a national newspaper entitled 'Sir Humphrey Needs to Learn Whose Boss'.[33] The former Education Minister, David Laws, argued officials were incapable of original policy thinking. Special advisers were needed:

> To lead the debate challenging both civil servants who are often not very good at doing more than following steers and aren't used to the idea that they are supposed to be thinking themselves.[34]

The civil service was deferential, going along with Ministers: 'My concern was that it was too passive in the face of a general ministerial direction and therefore afraid of serving up things it didn't think would be welcome'.[35] Another appointee attests:

> The civil service has been very reactive and often fails to get ahead of the game. They do very little scenario-planning or analysis and so they are often ill-prepared. Ministers used to get really frustrated because they wanted the civil service to come up with lots of ideas, but they just couldn't provide them.[36]

An aide who worked in the Department for Business, Innovation and Skills (BIS) insisted the problem with civil servants, 'wasn't the calibre, it was the turnover'[37]:

> After the 2010 election...the turnover of civil servants working on higher education was accelerated by austerity-related re-organisations and reduc-

[32] Transcript, David Laws, March 2016, Ministers reflect Archive, Institute for Government, Online: http://www.instituteforgovernment.org.uk/ministers-reflect/person/david-laws/ Accessed 30 September 2016.

[33] https://www.thetimes.co.uk/article/sir-humphrey-needs-to-learn-whos-the-boss-rjz96g53f Accessed 2nd February 2018.

[34] Transcript, David Laws, March 2016, Ministers reflect Archive, Institute for Government, Online: http://www.instituteforgovernment.org.uk/ministers-reflect/person/david-laws/ Accessed 30 September 2016.

[35] Transcript, David Laws, March 2016, Ministers reflect Archive, Institute for Government, Online: http://www.instituteforgovernment.org.uk/ministers-reflect/person/david-laws/ Accessed 30 September 2016.

[36] Interview with former Head of the Prime Minister's Delivery Unit (PMDU), April 19th 2012.

[37] Interview with a departmental special adviser, 20th October 2016.

tions in staff. In the crucial three months between August 2010 and October 2010—during which the independent review of Higher Education Funding and Student Finance completed its work, submitted its report to Government, and published its findings—BIS had three different people filling the Permanent Secretary role. There was no institutional memory on which to rely. (Hillman 2016: 331)

The state bureaucracy had 'systemic' flaws according to Nick Clegg (2016: 114):

The tendency for bright, young and wholly inexperienced officials to hold great sway over key areas of public policy for short periods of time, before being moved up the next rung of the ladder, creates discontinuity and immaturity in policy-making.

Maude's 2012 Plan echoed language used in the 1968 Fulton Report. Fulton observed:

One of the main troubles of the [Civil] Service has been that, in achieving immunity from political intervention, a system was evolved which until recently was virtually immune from outside pressures for change. Since it was not immune from inside resistance to change, inertia was perhaps predictable. (HMG 1968: 14)

The pressures to deliver policies effectively had also grown since the 1960s:

There are now more activist Ministers and advisers and this had led to challenges...the civil service has admitted that in a world of challenges a lot of the traditional civil service virtues were found wanting.[38]

The civil service outlook on the policy process was fundamentally flawed:

The model of change which still distorts a lot of policy-making assumes that pulling a lever at the top through a law or a programme actually has a series of effects. Most of the time it doesn't actually, particularly if you're concerned with schools or policing or hospitals.[39]

[38] Interview with Whitehall Think-Tank Director, 30th September 2016.
[39] Interview with the former Head of the Cabinet Office Strategy Unit (PMSU), February 16th 2012.

A review of the Whitehall system concurred: 'There have been criticisms of Civil Service capability. The Fulton Report description of policy officials being 'gifted amateurs' still has resonance'.[40] The 2012 document reiterated the civil service was characterised by, 'a culture that can seem slow-moving and hierarchical; where exceptional performance is too rarely recognised and underperformance not rigorously addressed'. Whitehall was, 'too often slow and resistant to change' (HMG 2012: 3–7). While Fulton glossed over the relationship between politicians and bureaucrats, the 2012 Plan indicated the 'governing marriage' ought to be revisited. According to a former permanent secretary, the political climate meant officials were less trusted:

As politics becomes more of a career and the role of the adviser is more of a professional career, there are greater incentives not to buy into the idea that civil servants are both competent and trustworthy. There was a decline in the starting-point of trust.[41]

The former Home Office Permanent Secretary, Sir David Normington, remarked:

I am concerned at what I see as a slow deterioration over time in the trust between Ministers and civil servants; with more willingness from Ministers to criticise civil servants in public; more leaks from within the Civil Service; a greater tendency to hold civil servants at arm's length and not to form with them the close partnership on which effective Government relies.[42]

Reformers including Maude and Oliver Letwin accepted talented officials provided Ministers with a 'Rolls-Royce' service. But they argued the system was broken. The permanent bureaucracy was dysfunctional and unwieldy.[43] Maude, Gove and Letwin believed the Whitehall machinery blocked ministerial initiatives it disliked. Officials would only get behind policies if they realised the consequences of not doing so were irrelevance.

[40] https://civilservicelearning.civilservice.gov.uk/sites/default/files/twelve_actions_report_web_accessible.pdf Accessed 16th March 2017.
[41] Interview with a former departmental permanent secretary, 19th October 2016.
[42] Cited in https://publications.parliament.uk/pa/cm201617/cmselect/cmpubadm/253/253.pdf Accessed 2nd February 2018.
[43] Interview with Whitehall Think-Tank research fellow, 12th December 2017.

Incoming Ministers believed the policy-making structures of Whitehall were ineffectual. As one civil servant admitted:

> In a digital age, traditional policy-making is largely broken. It is slow, inflexible, unnecessarily complicated, afraid of technology and afraid of change. The cycle of green paper, white paper, draft bill, and secondary legislation is no longer the best way to decide to create or develop new services because user needs are given scant consideration, however necessary the process may be for Parliament.[44]

The civil service 'monopoly' over policy advice was aggressively challenged. The growth of advisers was no doubt important Political advisers ensure a 'funnelling effect'; options are discarded if they are perceived to be politically damaging; proposals are inflicted on officials of which they were previously unaware; politicians bring experts into policy-making who were not vetted by officials; advisers work with Ministers to ensure departments are not 'captured' by vested interests; advisers undermine official advice (Eichbaum and Shaw 2007: 456). The civil service is in danger of being pushed to the margins.

Iain Duncan Smith's tenure at the Department of Work and Pensions (DWP) was instructive. IDS was appointed in 2010. He brought into DWP advisers and ideas from an independent think-tank, the Centre for Social Justice (CSJ); the CSJ was developing the concept of universal credit.[45] Civil servants had to take responsibility for implementing the universal credit proposals, a programme Whitehall played no role in devising. Because officials were determined to demonstrate loyalty to Duncan-Smith, flaws were too readily dismissed. Similarly, the Government's 'Troubled Families Programme', a response to disorder in English cities in 2011, was shaped by erroneous assumptions about, 'who 'troubled families' are, what causes their behaviour, and how to stop it', a classic instance of 'Policy-Based Evidence' (PBE); civil servants were never allowed to test the propositions underlying the programme before Ministers rushed to implementation (Cairney 2018: 5).

Increasingly, Ministers enter office with, 'an ideational policy portfolio in that they have their own strong priorities on what policy change is needed' (Richardson 2017: 12). Ministers are 'policy initiators'; policies are agreed

[44] http://mikebracken.com/blog/on-policy-and-delivery/ Accessed 15 December 2017.
[45] https://www.instituteforgovernment.org.uk/blog/problems-universal-credit Accessed 12th December 2017.

without civil servants being present. As a consequence, robust challenge is absent and there is little effort to identify hitches or complications (Sausman and Locke 2004). The Weberian bureaucracy emphasises the 'depersonalisation' of public policy. Policy-making is concerned with the 'administration of the public realm' rather than the whims of individual Ministers or political advisers (Clarke and Newman 1997). Nowadays, however, Ministers pursue their own agendas driving personal initiatives through the policy process.

The post-2010 governments were prepared to disrupt the civil service 'monopoly' in the name of 'open' policy-making. The monopoly had, of course, been weakening since the 1960s. The concept of the 'policy advisory system' was devised by William Plowden and developed by the Australian scholar, John Halligan, to denote the 'interlocking set of actors' who increasingly shape knowledge and policy advice (Craft and Howlett 2012: 80; Halligan 1995). Policy advice is a diverse 'marketplace' of institutions and policy entrepreneurs (Craft and Howlett 2012: 84). As a consequence, policy-making, 'has become a very large game which almost any number can play'; drawing on the work of the American political scientist, Charles O. Jones, Peters attests a shift has taken place from 'cosy little triangles' of decision-making dominated by traditional elites to 'big sloppy hexagons' of actors from 'inside' and 'outside' government (Peters 2000; cited in Gouglas 2016: 3). The literature emphasises the heterogeneity and complexity of advice in the Anglophone countries (Halligan 1995; Craft and Halligan 2015: 3; Fraussen and Halpin 2016: 117).

The Cameron governments openly attacked the civil service monopoly. The 2012 Plan announced a £500 million fund urging departments to enact 'contestable' policy-making. The intention was to:

> Commission high quality advice from outside the civil service on Ministers' priority areas; draw directly on the thinking, evidence and insight of external experts; and achieve a potentially broader and more radical range of options than Ministers would receive internally.[46]

As a result, 'external sources are given the opportunity, through competition, to develop policy' (House of Commons 2013). The former Cabinet Secretary, Lord Turnbull, embraced the arrival of new actors:

---

[46] https://www.gov.uk/guidance/contestable-policy-fund Accessed 5th September 2016.

We [the civil service] no longer claim a monopoly over policy advice. We welcome the fact that we are much more open to ideas from think-tanks, consultancies, governments abroad, special advisers, and frontline practitioners. In developing policy, we not only consult more widely than we used to but involve outsiders to a far greater degree in the policy-making process [through] the extensive use of outside reviewers—Turner, Eddington, Sandler, Higgs, etc.[47]

Turnbull quoted his Australian counterpart, Peter Shergold: 'Let me make it clear that I extol the fact that public service policy advice is increasingly contested. I welcome it intellectually: our perspectives and strategies benefit from challenge. I also welcome it professionally, as a public servant'. Yet many civil servants were deeply troubled.

THE CONTESTABLE POLICY FUND

The CPF was administered by the Cabinet Office 'Open Policy-Making Team'. The Institute for Public Policy Research (IPPR) were commissioned to carry out the first assignment, examining options for civil service reform.[48] An official concluded, 'Maude did not trust the civil service to do the work'.[49] Maude insisted: 'The IPPR review is a step towards our goal of policy-making being open by default and drawing on knowledge and insights from beyond Whitehall'.[50] The IPPR was instructed to provide, 'a detailed and substantial evidence-based review and assessment of government machinery in other countries and multilateral organisations', with the aim of developing, 'a range of specific options and recommendations for further reform of the British Civil Service...that explore alternative models of government to the Northcote-Trevelyan model, as well as any recommendations that build on the existing model'.[51]

[47] https://www.theguardian.com/politics/2005/jul/27/Whitehall.uk Accessed 14th December 2017.

[48] https://www.gov.uk/government/uploads/system/uploads/attachment_data/file/207237/Accountability_and_Responsiveness_in_the_SCS.pdf Accessed 5th September 2016.

[49] Interview with former Treasury and Cabinet Office official, 11th January 2018.

[50] https://www.gov.uk/government/news/government-s-first-use-of-contestable-policy-fund Accessed 12th January 2018. The review cost the Government £50,000; half was made available through the CPF; the remainder of the funding was provided by the Cabinet Office.

[51] Cited in: https://publications.parliament.uk/pa/cm201314/cmselect/cmpubadm/74/7406.htm Accessed 12th January 2018.

Six recommendations emerged: the Prime Minister should be given a formal say in the appointment of senior civil servants; Ministers must be allowed to create 'Extended Ministerial Offices'; the Head of the Civil Service should manage the performance of permanent secretaries; new permanent secretaries must be given time-limited four-year contracts; civil servants should answer directly to Parliament on operational matters; officials should advise the opposition parties prior to elections.[52]

In total, 18 projects were delivered under the CPF between 2012 and 2015.[53] Up to 2015, the fund was under-spent and not widely used (Rutter 2013). Departments were outsourcing analytical policy work already without the CPF's prompting.

The Institute for Government (IfG) note that opening-up Whitehall policy-making is not unprecedented; Royal Commissions, 'in which an array of the great and the good deliberated for years to come up with magisterial solutions', were replaced by speedier 'celebrity reviews', including the Dilnot review of social care, 'where a big name was asked to do a quick-fire study at the behest of Ministers'; 'arms-length' public bodies were established such as the Low Pay Commission to give specific advice.[54]

The impact of the CPF was nonetheless profound. The mind-set of officials was altered encouraging them to become, 'enablers and expert process designers rather than trying to monopolise policy-making input behind closed doors'.[55] Maude envisaged civil servants should 'manage' the process while Ministers shaped policy in consultation with advisers from think-tanks and management consultancies; officials would lose influence to the new breed of 'policy entrepreneurs' in the British state (Richardson 2017: 12).

Maude's view was civil servants should focus on operations and delivery rather than intellectual inputs to policy-making (Aucoin 2012). As a consequence, officials felt 'significantly marginalised' according to media reports (Waller 2012). The deteriorating relationship between permanent secretaries and Ministers was, 'the critical fracture point in the Civil Service

[52] https://www.gov.uk/government/uploads/system/uploads/attachment_data/file/207237/Accountability_and_Responsiveness_in_the_SCS.pdf Accessed 12th January 2018.

[53] https://www.gov.uk/guidance/contestable-policy-fund Accessed 5th September 2016.

[54] https://www.instituteforgovernment.org.uk/sites/default/files/publications/opening_up%20policy%20making_final.pdf Accessed 20th December 2017.

[55] https://www.instituteforgovernment.org.uk/sites/default/files/publications/opening_up%20policy%20making_final.pdf Accessed 20th December 2017.

structure'.[56] Although 'one shouldn't go to the opposite extreme and say civil servants don't matter...The monopoly [over policy-making] has ended'.[57] 'The civil service does retain a role', but it is confined to, 'turning ideas into practical policy'.[58] Officials must drive ministerial policy initiatives with conviction, delivering targets prescribed by politicians (Richardson 2017; Richards and Smith 2016).

The IfG think-tank warned of the dangers of undermining the Whitehall model: 'Contrary to the popular narrative', over the last eight years the Civil Service has broadly said, 'yes, Minister'; 'the Civil Service has willingly taken on extreme levels of risk in support of ministerial agendas'.[59] There are fewer checks and balances. The executive is more controlling and powerful than ever. The constitutional independence of the civil service has been belittled by successive governments with damaging implications. Despite a decade of devolution, British government is a 'power-hoarding system' where authority is amassed in Whitehall. Little effort is made to consult actors beyond the central state. Ministers affirm their autonomy by reducing structural dependence on bureaucrats.

What caused the civil service 'monopoly' to break down? While officials were under attack, new actors emerged to fill the void. Outside government there were think-tanks, NGOs, and management consultancies; the development of technical competences and specialist analytical skills beyond Whitehall; and a growing tendency for governments to 'externalise' responsibility, creating independent central banks and arms-length bodies with a mandate of operational independence (Halligan 1995; Craft and Halligan 2015: 3; Burnham 2002). The externalisation of policy advice and the growth of outside bodies contributed towards the fragmentation of policy-making (Van den Berg 2016).

At Ministers' insistence, the supply of policy advice has widened beyond the civil service while political goals are enforced throughout (Craft and Halligan 2015: 3). The new actors in British government are the 'entrepreneurs of the state' committed to the partisan imperatives of the Minister who recruited them (Leys 2006). Externalisation and politicisation are

---

[56] https://publications.parliament.uk/pa/cm201617/cmselect/cmpubadm/253/253.pdf Accessed 2nd February 2018.

[57] Interview with former Head of a Whitehall think-tank, 30th September 2016.

[58] Interview with a senior official in the Department for Education and the Ministry of Justice, 7th October 2016.

[59] https://civilservant.org.uk/library/2014_IfG_Leading_Change.pdf Accessed 20th December 2017. Cited in Richardson 2017: 14.

linked; political advisers are sceptical of official guidance and 'broker' advice, maintaining contacts with researchers in ideologically sympathetic consultancies and think-tanks (Eichbaum and Shaw 2007; Stoker and Gains 2011). As Stoker and Gains (2011) and Page (2010) recount, special advisers do not lead inevitably to politicisation. It is influence that matters. Special advisers are channels through which external actors penetrate the hitherto closed policy-making structures of the British state.

Particular attention is paid to think-tanks as 'proactive policy pioneers' (Fraussen and Halpin 2016: 117). Think-tanks bridge the worlds of 'ideas, analysis and action'; they acquire influence as the prestige of universities has declined; political parties and trade unions are less focused on research; think-tanks fill the vacuum, 'constructing the frameworks within which policy problems are understood' (Bentham 2006: 170; Mulgan 2006: 149; Stone 2006; Denham and Garnett 2006). There are critics who argue think-tanks present themselves, 'as legitimate and trustworthy sources of value-free advice to decision-makers'; think-tanks engage in, 'a game of gathering, balancing, and assembling various institutionalised forms of capital, especially academic, political, economic and media capital' (Medvetz cited in Shaw et al. 2015: 73).

Management consultants exert greater influence in Whitehall too; reports indicate spending on consultants has risen significantly since the 1980s.[60] There is evidence of a 'consultocracy' where consultants side-line 'publicly accountable' officials in shaping government's priorities (Gunter et al. 2015). Over the last thirty years, 'public policy makers have increased their use of management consulting knowledge in reforming their bureaucracies' (Saint-Martin 1998: 41). NPM reforms encouraged governments to recruit consultants; consultants are used for 'process support' alongside policy advice (Van den Berg 2016: 72). Morgan and Sturdy (2017) chart the influence of management consultancies in shaping global public policies. Consultancies are implicated in the marketization of the public sector. British government is dominated by this cadre of unelected advisers who have little concern for due process or democratic legitimacy (Leys 2006).

[60] https://www.ft.com/content/2517019c-b93a-11e5-bf7e-8a339b6f2164   Accessed 15th December 2017.

MINISTERIAL-CIVIL SERVICE RELATIONSHIPS: MUTUAL DEPENDENCY AND INSTITUTIONAL RESILIENCE?

Despite evidence the Whitehall model is unravelling, it is nevertheless claimed that relationships between Ministers and civil servants remain respectful, whatever the influence of advisers and think-tanks. Iain Duncan-Smith contends: 'Ministers and civil servants need to work closely together for problem solving'.[61] Martin Donnelly, former Permanent Secretary at the Department for Business, Innovation and Science (BIS) concurs:

> It is not a given that an incoming Minister, perhaps of a different political party, probably of a different temperament and outlook from her or his predecessor, should immediately trust official advice. To add value for Ministers across government requires the foundation of a relationship of mutual trust, built on professional respect, and evidence of competence, and able to handle the pressure of events.

There are some who argue during the Coalition years, the civil service built constructive links with Ministers (Waller 2012). One observer of the machine concluded having interviewed Ministers, 'What comes across is their respect for civil servants'.[62] In the face of a more volatile environment shaped by the rise of 'anti-politics' and the emergence of 'post-truth' democracy, Ministers and civil servants stuck together:

> Trust is getting more problematic and difficult. Ministers and officials are often on the same side. The problem is a feral media. The media blow things up...Ministers want to respond in ways that aren't helpful. 24-hour news has made maintaining trust that much harder. Camilla Batmanghelidjh and Kids Company [show] it is very difficult. You are working in a very unsympathetic environment. It is very difficult to have a nuanced policy debate. Time horizons and trust come together. Civil servants have become more of a target for the media...the press view is that the public sector is incompetent and nasty.[63]

The impact of special advisers is thus believed to be exaggerated. Competent advisers support the civil service by offering insight while

---

[61] Interview with Whitehall Think-Tank Director, 30th September 2016.
[62] Interview with Whitehall Think-Tank Director, 30th September 2016.
[63] Interview with former departmental permanent secretary, 19th October 2016.

keeping officials abreast of their Minister's views. Political appointees guarantee the independence of civil servants, undertaking tasks on Ministers' behalf. The Cameron Administration 'empowered' mandarins by emphasising evidence-based policy-making; Ministers enforced, 'a return to due process in terms of collective policy clearance' (Hazell 2012: 67). There was investment in 'evidence institutions' and the network of 'what works' centres, 'to make better decisions'.[64] The admiration for constitutional convention was apparent in Oliver Letwin's speech to the IfG heaping praise on the British administrative class:

> I observed Robert Armstrong's Rolls-Royce minutes gliding across from the cabinet office; I listened to Robin Butler and Charles Powell manage the affairs of a great Prime Minister; I witnessed the calm efficiency with which Michael Scholar, Andrew Turnbull, David Norgrove and others despatched the business of government from the private office. These fine officials made me understand a great deal about what an administrative civil service ought to be. Then, as now, the virtues these officials displayed were not universal—but they provided a model of the thing at its best. (Letwin 2012)

Moreover, the number of advisers appointed in countries in the Westminster tradition was tiny in comparison to the 'spoils system' operating in the United States (Qvortrup 2005).

Disputes between officials and Ministers have long existed. The relationship between civil servants and Ministers was never wholly cordial; for instance, the clash between Richard Crossman and his permanent secretary, Dame Evelyn Sharpe, was legendary; Roy Jenkins sacked one of his officials in the Home Office who was perceived to be reactionary.[65] Jeremy Heywood's seniority in Number Ten symbolised the continuing influence of the civil service. As one observer concluded:

> That to me look[ed] like a classic 1970s Cabinet Secretary role of the kind that appears in Bernard Donoughue's diaries. The Cabinet Secretary is the powerbroker in Whitehall and is there to do the Prime Minister's bidding.[66]

---

[64] https://www.psa.ac.uk/insight-plus/making-better-use-evidence-government Accessed 18th January 2018.

[65] Interview with former Head of the Number Ten Policy Unit, 12th February 2012.

[66] Interview with former Head of the Number Ten Policy Unit, 12th February 2012.

Although the Cabinet Secretary's role was split in 2011 and Bob Kerslake became Head of the Civil Service (as well as Permanent Secretary at the Department of Communities and Local Government), Heywood retained authority in Number Ten (Haddon 2016). Under Cameron's governments, political advisers received instructions not to 'throw their weight around'; they were told by permanent secretaries:

> Those New Labour special advisers were far too powerful; don't get above yourselves, you're here to serve the department; they were sending us a warning shot. The irony was that…after having squelched us when we arrived, they called us back in and said, 'why aren't you throwing your weight around Whitehall more on behalf of the department?'[67]

'[Special advisers] retreated a certain amount compared with the breadth of influence they enjoyed under Labour' (Waller 2012: 79). The Prime Minister's view reflected Donnelly's (2014: 7) assessment: 'The crucial specificity of the British system is that political or personal advisers are not a separate layer of administration'. Many advisers, 'lacked experience of government, and did not have the confidence or authority to negotiate on behalf of their Ministers' (Hazell 2012: 64). The Prime Minister made clear he did not want advisers to exploit disagreements between civil servants and Ministers.

CONCLUSION

Despite those caveats, this chapter contends officials are being removed from their legitimate role in the policy-making process. Bureaucrats believe they have been dislodged from their position as ministerial confidents. Guidance on policy from officials raising awkward questions is disparaged or vilified. Civil servants have to translate policies they played no role in devising into workable programmes. Where embarrassing 'blunders' occur, officials are blamed. The mutual dependency between Ministers and officials has atrophied. Undoubtedly, the growth of special advisers has been significant. Advisory staff have different motives and use the authority of Ministers to shape policies. They undermine the nonpartisan ethos of the state bureaucracy. The growing influence of think-tanks and management consultancies has been equally important.

[67] Interview with a departmental special adviser, 20th October 2016.

Officials know if they fail to satisfy politicians' demands, they will be pushed out. Cameron's Ministers insisted civil servants had to be imaginative and embrace risk-taking. They had to convey passion and enthusiasm about government initiatives. The distinction between 'politics' and 'administration' at the heart of Weber's view of rational 'ideal-type' bureaucracy was being eroded. Civil servants were expected not only to understand politics, but to think and behave in partisan terms. Officials were part of the 'permanent campaign' machine that bolstered the governing party's legitimacy. Those who did not co-operate were aware Ministers no longer valued well-informed advice for its own sake. The influence of the civil service establishment was waning. The shrinking capacity of Whitehall provided yet more impetus to seek expertise from elsewhere.[68]

BIBLIOGRAPHY

Aucoin, P. (2012). New Political Governance in Westminster Systems: Impartial Public Administration and Management Performance at Risk. *Governance, 25*(2), 177–199.

Bakvis, H., & Jarvis, M. (Eds.). (2012). Introduction: Peter C. Aucoin: From New Public Management to New Political Governance. In *From New Public Management to New Political Governance*. McGill-Queens University Press.

Balogh, T. (1959). The Apotheosis of the Dilettente. In H. Thomas (Ed.), *Crisis in the Civil Service*. London: Blond.

Bentham, J. (2006). The IPPR and Demos: Think-Tanks of the New Social Democracy. *Political Quarterly, 77*(2), 166–176.

Blick, A. (2004). *People Who Live in the Dark: The History of the Special Adviser in British Politics*. London: Politico's.

Burnham, P. (2002). New Labour and the Politics of Depoliticisation. *British Journal of Politics and International Relations, 3*(2), 127–149.

Cairney, P. (2018). The UK Government's Imaginative Use of Evidence to Make Policy. *British Politics*, Forthcoming.

Clarke, J., & Newman, J. (1997). *The Managerial State*. London: Sage.

Clegg, N. (2016). *Politics: Between the Extremes*. London: Bodley Head.

Craft, J. (2013). Appointed Political Staffs and the Diversification of Policy Advisory Sources: Theory and Evidence from Canada. *Policy and Society, 32*(3), 211–223.

---

[68] https://www.civilserviceworld.com/articles/news/gus-attacks-outsourcing-policy-advice Accessed 15th December 2017.

Craft, J., & Halligan, J. (2015, July 1–4). *Looking Back and Thinking Ahead: 30 Years of Policy Advisory System Scholarship.* Prepared for T08P06 Comparing Policy Advisory Systems. International Conference on Public Policy. Catholic University of Sacro Cuore, Milan.

Craft, J., & Howlett, M. (2012). Policy Formulation, Governance Shifts and Policy Influence: Location and Content in Policy Advisory Systems. *Journal of Public Policy, 32*(2), 79–98.

Denham, A., & Garnett, M. (2006). What Works? British Think-Tanks and the 'End of Ideology'. *Political Quarterly, 77*(2), 156–165.

Donnelly, M. (2014, June 30). Speech to the Institute of Government.

Eichbaum, C., & Shaw, R. (2007). Ministerial Advisers and the Politics of Policy-Making: Bureaucratic Permanence and Popular Control. *Australian Journal of Public Administration, 66*(4), 453–467.

Fraussen, B., & Halpin, D. (2016). Think Tanks and Strategic Policymaking: The Contribution of Think Tanks to Policy Advisory Systems. *Policy Sciences, 50*(1), 105–124.

Gains, F., & Stoker, G. (2011). Special Advisers and the Transmission of Ideas from the Primeval Policy Soup. *Policy and Politics, 39*(4), 485–498(14).

Gouglas, A. (2016). *Paper Drafted for Internal Use in View of the Preparation for a KU Leuven OT Project on 'Policy Advice Utilisation in European Policy Advisory Systems'.* KU Leuven Public Management Institute.

Gouglas, A., & Brans, M. (2016, February 9). *UK Extended Ministerial Offices: On the Road to Cabinetisation?* London: Constitution Unit Blog. https://constitution-unit.com/2016/02/09/uk-extended-ministerial-offices-on-the-road-to-cabinetisation/

Grube, D. (2015). Responsibility to Be Enthusiastic? Public Servants and the Public Face of 'Promiscuous Partisanship'. *Governance, 28*(3), 305–320.

Gunter, H. M., Hall, D., & Mills, C. (2015). Consultants, Consultancy and Consultocracy in Education Policymaking in England. *Journal of Education Policy, 30*(4), 518–539.

Haddon, C. (2016). Developments in the Civil Service. In R. Heffernan, C. Hay, M. Russell, & P. Cowley (Eds.), *Developments in British Politics 10.* Basingstoke: Palgrave Macmillan.

Halligan, J. (1995). Policy Advice and the Public Sector. In B. G. Peters & D. T. Savoie (Eds.), *Governance in a Changing Environment* (pp. 138–172). Montreal: McGill-Queen's University Press.

Hazell, R. (2012). How the Coalition Works at the Centre. In R. Hazell & B. Yong (Eds.), *The Politics of Coalition: How the Conservative-Liberal Democrat Government Works.* Oxford: Hart Publishing.

Her Majesty's Government (HMG). (1968). *The Civil Service: Report of the Committee Chaired by Lord Fulton.* London: HMG.

Her Majesty's Government (HMG). (2012). *Civil Service Reform Plan*. London: HMG.

Hillman, N. (2016). The Coalition's Higher Education Reforms in England. *Oxford Review of Education, 42*(3), 330–345.

Letwin, O. (2012, September 17). *Why Mandarins Matter: Keynote Speech*. London: Institute for Government.

Leys, C. (2006). The Cynical State. In *The Socialist Register*. London: Merlin Press.

Morgan, G., & Sturdy, A. (2017). The Role of Large Management Consultancy Firms in Global Public Policy. In D. Stone & K. Maloney (Eds.), *Oxford Handbook on Global Public Policy and Transnational Administration*. Oxford: Oxford University Press.

Mulgan, G. (2006). Thinking in Tanks: The Changing Ecology of Political Ideas. *Political Quarterly, 77*(2), 147–155.

Niskanen, W. A. (1994). *Bureaucracy and Public Economics*. Vermont: Edward Elgar Publishing.

O'Malley, M. (2017). Temporary Partisans, Tagged Officers or Impartial Professionals: Moving Between Ministerial Offices and Departments. *Public Administration, 95*(1), 407–420.

Page, E. (2010). Has the Whitehall Model Survived? *International Journal of Administrative Sciences, 76*(3), 407–423.

Peters, B. G. (2000). *The Future of Governing* (2nd ed.). Lawrence: University Press of Kansas.

Peters, G., & Pierre, J. (2004). *Politicisation of the Civil Service in Comparative Perspective: The Quest for Control*. London: Routledge.

Peters, G.-P., & Savoie, D. (1994). Civil Service Reform: Misdiagnosing the Patient. *Public Administration Review, 54*(5), 418–425.

Qvortrup, M. (2005). *Memorandum to the Select Committee on Public Administration – Written Evidence*. London: House of Commons.

Rhodes, R. A. W. (2011a). *Everyday Life in British Government*. Oxford: Oxford University Press.

Rhodes, R. A. W. (2011b). One-Way, Two-Way, or Dead-End Street: The British Influence on American Public Administration. *Public Administration Review, 74*(4), 559–571.

Richards, D., & Smith, M. (2016). The Westminster Model and the 'Indivisibility of the Political and Economic Elite': A Convenient Myth Whose Time Is up? *Governance, 29*(4), 499–516.

Richardson, J. (2017). The Changing British Policy Style: From Governance to Government? *British Politics*, Forthcoming.

Rutter, J. (2013, June 19). Ministers Should Commission IPPR and Civil Service Advice in Parallel. *The Guardian*.

Saint-Martin, D. (1998). Les consultants et la réforme managérialiste de l'État en France et en Grande-Bretagne: vers l'émergence d'une 'consultocratie'? *Revue canadienne de science politique, 32*(1), 41–74.

Sausman, C., & Locke, R. (2004). The British Civil Service: Examining the Question of Politicisation. In G. B. Peters & J. Pierre (Eds.), *Politicisation of the Civil Service in Comparative Perspective* (pp. 101–124). London: Routledge.

Shaw, S. E., Russell, J., Parsons, W., & Greenhalgh, T. (2015). The View from Nowhere? How Think-Tanks Work to Shape Health Policy. *Critical Policy Studies, 9*(1), 58–77.

Stone, D. (2006). Think-Tanks and Policy Analysis. In F. Fischer, G. J. Miller, & M. S. Sidney (Eds.), *Handbook of Public Policy Analysis: Theory, Methods and Politics* (pp. 149–157). New York: Marcel Dekker Inc.

Van den Berg, C. (2016). Dynamics in the Dutch Policy Advisory System: Externalisation, Politicisation and the Legacy of Pillarisation. *Policy Sciences, 50*(1), 63–84.

Waller, P. (2012). Departments: Ministers and the Civil Service. In R. Hazell & B. Yong (Eds.), *The Politics of Coalition: How the Conservative-Liberal Democrat Government Works*. Oxford: Hart Publishing.

Wildavsky, A. (1979). *Speaking Truth to Power: The Art and Craft of Policy Analysis*. New York: Little Brown.

Yong, B., & Hazell, R. (2014). *Special Advisers: What They Do and Why They Matter*. London: Bloomsbury.

CHAPTER 4

The Personalisation of Appointments

INTRODUCTION

Over the last decade, the institutions and practices of the Whitehall model have been radically altered by the growth of political appointees and the erosion of the civil service 'monopoly' over policy advice. The argument of the book is two-fold. Firstly, the Whitehall 'paradigm' is being transformed to the point where it is barely recognisable from what emerged in the aftermath of the Second World War. Secondly, the changes are scarcely conducive to good government. It is true the model had to change given new technologies and the demand for 'user-led' services. But important constitutional and administrative principles have been sacrificed, endangering the efficacy of British governance. As if this wasn't enough, after 2010 sustained effort was made not only to bring in appointees and challenge officials' monopoly over policy advice, but to 'personalise' civil service careers.

The principle of appointment on merit is at the core of the Whitehall paradigm. Merit-based appointment was not only intended to attract the 'brightest and the best' into the British civil service. Following the Northcote-Trevelyan reforms, officials no longer depended on ministerial patronage. The domestic civil service was recruited via competitive examination on the basis of merit, 'rather than as had hitherto been the case, on the basis of patronage, connection, inertia and seniority' (Cannadine 2017: 296). Civil servants were confident they could speak the truth without being dismissed: 'you can

© The Author(s) 2019
P. Diamond, *The End of Whitehall?*,
https://doi.org/10.1007/978-3-319-96101-9_4

give objective advice without losing your job'.[1] David Cannadine (2017: 296) contends Northcote-Trevelyan forged, 'a new mandarin caste: university educated, literate, incorruptible and apolitical, and pervaded by a tone of impartial public-spiritedness'.

There is evidence the Northcote-Trevelyan settlement is being undermined. In his work on the New Political Governance (NPG), Aucoin observes that in the Anglophone democracies, Ministers are intervening to influence the appointment of civil servants. In the UK, both Cameron and May sought a formal role in the appointment of permanent secretaries. The evidence is officials who lose the confidence of Ministers are likely to be removed. As a consequence, civil service careers are more fluid; officials are dependent on ministerial patronage as never before.

At the heart of these changes are governance ideas, in particular 'principle-agent' theory that defined the first wave of New Public Management (NPM) reforms. Derived from economic doctrines popularised by the New Right, 'principle-agent' theory held that bureaucrats had to be controlled since they had their own vested interests. Public servants were self-interested, inclined to maximise their status and power.[2] That idea is alive thirty years later and, 'underscores the mutually reinforcing effect of ideas and institutions' (Beland and Cox 2011: 9). The personalisation of appointments is another means by which Ministers shape bureaucratic behaviour and exert greater control over the state machinery. This chapter will focus on the extent to which civil service appointments have been 'personalised' since 2010. The evidence is the notion of a permanent career in Whitehall is being undermined, even if there is as yet little indication of a wholesale political 'purge' of the civil service (Sausman and Locke 2004).

Civil Servants: Pleasing Their Political Masters?

In the Anglophone countries, there are concerns the line between 'administration' and 'politics' has blurred (O'Malley 2017: 407). As a consequence, civil service roles are being politicised (Aucoin 2012). It is important to stress personalisation and politicisation are not the same. Yet if the careers

---

[1] https://www.gresham.ac.uk/lectures-and-events/the-civil-service-and-the-constitution Accessed 19th December 2017.

[2] The theory of 'bureau-shaping' was developed by Professor Patrick Dunleavy in response to New Right ideas about budget maximisation.

of officials depend on the approval of Ministers, civil servants have little choice but to comply with partisan goals. To be rewarded with preferment, officials must be 'enthusiastic' about the government's agenda (Bakvis and Jarvis 2012: 16). In this climate, 'senior civil servants now look to the Prime Minister's court for making it to the top' (Savoie 2008: 17). Politicians want officials around them committed to the success of their policies.

Britain is not the only mature democracy where the meritocratic principle is being undermined. In Australia, for instance, personalisation of careers was formalised in the late 1980s as governments imposed contracts on 'departmental secretaries' (Qvortrup 2005). In New Zealand, 'chief executives' are appointed on four-year performance-based arrangements (Aucoin 2012). In Australia, the machinery of government is politically controlled while civil servants perceive themselves to be 'personal agents' of Ministers; in New Zealand, officials are held to account by targets (Paun and Harris 2012: 3). The New Zealand system permits experimentation since ideas readily permeate the structures of government; but there is concern about the fragmentation of delivery and the narrowing of the deliberative space for policy-making.[3]

In the Whitehall model, Ministers and civil servants worked together as the distinction between 'politics' and 'administration' is maintained. NPG overturns the separation of administration from politics. Civil servants comply with the goals of Ministers engaged in a 'permanent campaign' to achieve electoral ascendency for the governing party. Officials struggle to give dispassionate advice to Ministers or point out favoured policies are flawed. As the *Better Government Initiative* commented, 'Civil servants cannot be expected to give frank advice which disagrees with the Minister, or which challenges advice from a Special Adviser or favoured external think-tank, if that advice is likely to prove career limiting'.[4] The desire for advancement means officials are all too eager to please their political masters. More than a decade ago, the Hutton Inquiry set up to investigate the circumstances surrounding the death of the government scientist, Dr David Kelly found, 'senior civil servants may be unconsciously influenced by contacts with Downing Street—a desire to be helpful and to please'.[5]

---

[3] http://www.civilservant.org.uk/index.html#reform Accessed 6th February 2016.
[4] http://www.bettergovernmentinitiative.co.uk/wp-content/uploads/2013/07/Civil-Service-final.pdf Accessed 18th December 2017.
[5] https://fas.org/irp/world/uk/huttonreport.pdf Accessed 18th November 2017.

Another casualty of personalisation is reciprocal trust between officials and Ministers. The mutual dependency affirmed by Haldane that shaped the post-war 'governing marriage' has broken down. Officials depend on winning the approval of Ministers. But politicians are less reliant on civil servants. Ministers are able to build up an 'entourage' of staff separate from the permanent bureaucracy, loyal to them personally. The core assumption that officials would be recruited to a 'job for life' on merit has been overturned. The personalisation of appointments is a further disruption to the Whitehall 'paradigm'.

The Civil Service Appointments Process

Personalisation did not begin during Cameron's premiership. 'Irregular' appointments grew under the Blair governments. Michael Barber who was David Blunkett's adviser as Secretary of State for Education and Skills was appointed Head of the Prime Minister's Delivery Unit in 2001 through open competition; although Barber was recruited according to established protocol, his affiliation with the Labour party made it unlikely he would be retained by an incoming Conservative government.[6] Barber's appointment amounted to a blurring of the line between 'politics' and 'administration', tacitly undermining the Northcote-Trevelyan principles. The Delivery Unit was a technocratic body, but run by an official with strong links to the governing party. As Hennessy remarks:

> The true test [of EMOs and ministerial involvement in permanent secretary appointments] will bite when a new Government of a different political colour takes office. If greater ministerial choice of Permanent Secretaries has happened and several EMOs are in place—especially if they have morphed into central directorates, essentially departments within departments—might not the new Secretaries of State feel that they are inheriting a senior Civil Service that has, to quite a high degree, been politicised? True, these new Ministers will be able to create their own EMOs afresh, but is there not a risk of a future Government saying no doubt, with regret, we must replace the senior career officials too with bespoke civil servants of our own choice? Should that happen, the Northcote-Trevelyan principles would effectively have been abandoned and our Civil Service will have passed through a one-way valve.[7]

⁶ https://www.theguardian.com/politics/2002/apr/09/Whitehall.uk Accessed 19th December 2017.
⁷ https://publications.parliament.uk/pa/ld201314/ldhansrd/text/140116-0001.htm Accessed 6th February 2018.

Changes to civil service appointments now appear irreversible. Incoming Ministers expect to handpick their officials and recruit their own team of advisers. If they don't like the Permanent Secretary running their department, that official is elbowed to one side. This situation undermines the established merit-based ethos and institutions of the British system of government. The Whitehall bureaucracy has passed through a critical juncture. We have reached a moment of breakdown where the fabric of British governance is being steadily unpicked from within.

Appointing Permanent Secretaries

Ministers seek greater influence over the appointment of Permanent Secretaries and Director-Generals. The urge to regain control reflected frustration with the bureaucratic machinery. As one adviser opined, 'Civil servants are just obstructive. There is a growing realisation that if you don't do stuff in the first two years of a term it just doesn't get done. We need to get on with things now. There's no time for a Whitehall-style box ticking risk assessment on everything'. After 2010, permanent secretaries were more likely to be replaced when a new Secretary of State was appointed. David Bell at the Department for Education moved after Gove's arrival as Secretary of State. Nicholas Macpherson at the Treasury was the only permanent secretary in 2015 in post five years previously; five departments appointed three permanent secretaries between 2010 and 2015 (Freeguard et al. 2015: 62). When May became Prime Minister, five permanent secretaries distrusted by her inner circle were removed (IfG 2018). The former Cabinet Secretary, Lord Butler, criticised the growing 'churn' (Agbonlahor 2013).

The political class sought to appoint a new breed of 'can-do' officials to the top posts.[8] David Normington felt this was, 'the thin end of the wedge towards politicisation'.[9] Cameron wanted the final decision on the appointment of mandarins; he argued Ministers had been too constrained in the past. Politicians were held back:

Rather excessively in recent years so that there is one name and the Prime Minister either has to say 'yes' or 'no'...I don't think we should have ended

---

[8] http://www.telegraph.co.uk/news/politics/9874960/Ministers-new-plan-to-steamroller-civil-servants.html Accessed 8th February 2018.

[9] Interview with a former departmental permanent secretary, 6th April 2018.

up in that position. It would have been better for one or two people to get over the line, as it were. Then the Prime Minister, in conversation with the Cabinet Secretary and perhaps the Secretary of State, to make the decision. I do not think that that's politicisation. I think that's just the ability of a government to make sure it's got the right people in place to carry out the government's policy.[10]

Cameron's proposal that the Prime Minister should select permanent secretaries from a shortlist was resisted by the Civil Service Commission. Ministers were increasingly exercising influence using, 'opaque and undocumented channels'; the IfG found:

Selection panels are known to take active steps to avoid the possibility of a veto—to the point of avoiding recommending a candidate likely to be opposed by the Minister. Selection competitions are also run in circumstances where it is more or less known in advance who the successful candidate will be. Managed moves offer another mechanism for undocumented ministerial influence.[11]

A Coalition adviser recalled three different permanent secretaries appointed to their department during the summer of 2010.[12] Another remarked: 'Permanent secretaries got moved on; there was quite a turnover in the 2010–2015 period'.[13] Maude claimed it was legitimate for officials to be handpicked by Ministers. Ministers were accountable to Parliament for the performance of their department. Politicians must have confidence in the Permanent Secretary. Before the 2012 Plan was published, Maude extolled the virtues of the New Zealand system (Paun et al. 2010). The final draft diluted proposals for ministerial involvement, despite the IPPR's recommendations. Whitehall was increasingly nervous and fought back.

Officials saw off proposals to give Ministers the final say in permanent secretary selection, although Ministers were no longer presented with a

---

[10] Cited in https://publications.parliament.uk/pa/ld201314/ldhansrd/text/140116-0001.htm Accessed 6th February 2018.

[11] http://civilservicecommission.independent.gov.uk/wp-content/uploads/2014/04/CB-13-31-ANNEX-IFG-Report.pdf Accessed 23rd February 2018.

[12] Interview with a departmental special adviser, 20th October 2016.

[13] Interview with Whitehall Think-Tank Director, 30th September 2016.

single candidate they could approve or reject (Normington 2013).[14] The Whitehall bureaucracy saw itself as the 'custodian' of the public interest, upholding the proprieties of the British constitution while protecting norms of non-partisanship and impartiality at the heart of the Northcote-Trevelyan tradition.[15] The 2012 Plan had no clear rationale, written by a committee comprising Maude, Heywood and Kerslake. Ultimately, the group did not agree on the purpose of reform.[16] The Public Administration Select Committee (PASC) argued the Plan failed to espouse, 'any comprehensive analysis of why some things are successful and some things go wrong in government, and why the civil service appears to find it so hard to learn from success and failure'.[17] The complaint among Ministers was the Plan identified failings, but its remedies were incremental and small-scale.[18] The PASC recommended a Royal Commission on the future of the civil service but the Cameron Government dismissed the proposal as a 'distraction'.[19]

Although officials moved on where the relationship with Ministers was an issue, some observers argued, 'it was ever thus', and, 'promotion by merit has always been a fallacy'.[20] Where officials were replaced, it was by civil servants, not 'outsiders'. Where permanent secretaries left their posts:

> The replacements were invariably career civil servants; for all the moaning, 'oh we want someone from outside', it was very seldom truly someone from outside. They've been people who've come in as Director-Generals or second permanent secretaries to do particular functions and then moved into the mainstream, like Stephen Lovegrove at Defence. He was regarded as someone who had learnt the ways of Whitehall…usually an insider or quasi-insider got the top jobs.[21]

[14] http://civilservicecommission.independent.gov.uk/wp-content/uploads/2014/04/CB-13-31-ANNEX-IFG-Report.pdf Accessed 7th March 2018.
[15] Interview with Whitehall Think-Tank Director, 30th September 2016.
[16] Interview with former Treasury and Cabinet Office official, 11th January 2018.
[17] https://publications.parliament.uk/pa/cm201617/cmselect/cmpubadm/253/253.pdf Accessed 2nd February 2018.
[18] http://www.civilservant.org.uk/index.html#reform Accessed 6th February 2016.
[19] http://www.civilservant.org.uk/index.html#reform Accessed 6th February 2016.
[20] Interview with Whitehall Think-Tank research fellow, 12th December 2017.
[21] Interview with Whitehall Think-Tank Director, 30th September 2016.

Although Lovegrove came from Deutsche Bank, officials were rarely swapped for genuine 'outsiders'. Whitehall remained notoriously reluctant to bring in external appointees.

RECRUITMENT BEYOND WHITEHALL

There is little doubt, however, that Whitehall became increasingly porous after 2010 with greater emphasis on external recruitment. The 'jobs for life' model was being undermined. External recruits were required to address skills-gaps in specialist areas of delivery, notably finance, public sector commissioning, human resources, technology, and procurement. One 'Whitehall watcher' remarked:

> The civil service has brought in people to run things, HMRC and social security, mainly because these are much more complicated organisations. What the state is trying to do is not as straight forward as in the past. If you are dealing with pensions the Attlee world was a very straight forward one... now it's a heavily discretionary state...[the civil service] has adapted slowly but it's adapted. At the top level, the policy level, they have brought in a lot of people...one shouldn't under-rate people coming from local government either.[22]

Bringing in outside talent was hardly revolutionary. After all, most posts were not exposed to external competition. Many permanent secretaries rose up the traditional career ladder. Thatcher began the process of recruiting private sector managers during the 1980s. The wartime coalition appointed 'irregulars' in the 1940s (Addison 1976). Back in the 1920s, Lloyd George's 'garden suburb' brought in prime ministerial appointees. The recruitment of 'outsiders' to senior posts in the state bureaucracy was not a radical break with past practice. That said the 'job for life' structure was breaking down. As one observer noted, 'The civil service is clearly different to thirty years ago. It is more diverse with a wider range of skills. It is opening up beyond the civil service to the wider public sector'.[23]

---

[22] Interview with a senior official in the Department for Education and the Ministry of Justice, 7th October 2016.
[23] Interview with Whitehall Think-Tank Director, 30th September 2016.

DEPARTMENTAL BOARDS

The culture of an insular civil service has thus been ebbing away. The integrity of Whitehall's institutions is under threat. Aucoin (2012: 194) pointed out departmental boards merging 'politics' and 'management' are a particular concern. Boards bring non-executive directors into departments, some of whom were prominent donors to the Conservative party (Shipman 2017: 158). Boards were championed by Maude; they are chaired by the Secretary of State alongside four non-executive directors, often from the private sector, underlining the influence of 'testosterone fuelled' NPM-style reforms.[24]

Departmental boards have a mandate to 'scrutinise delivery', monitoring business plans. In practice, Ministers take charge of departmental management, marginalising permanent secretaries; external appointees intervene in policy-making and implementation, influencing personnel and finance decisions (McClory 2010). John Manzoni from the private sector was appointed Chief Executive of the Civil Service in October 2014 with a mandate to improve recruitment and procurement. Manzoni was a former executive at British Petroleum (BP); despite being appointed to the civil service, Manzoni retained his role as non-executive Director of the alcoholic drinks company, SAB Miller.[25] Such reforms and changes further eroded the demarcation between 'administration' and 'politics'.

DEMORALISING THE CIVIL SERVICE

The 'winners-takes-all' nature of the British political system coupled with the unfettered power of the executive enables the governing party to impose personnel on the machine. One former permanent secretary admitted: 'Patronage got significantly worse after 2010 in appointments to public bodies and agencies'.[26] To enhance their chances of promotion, it was feared civil servants and public sector managers no longer 'spoke truth to power' (Wildavsky 1979). It is hard to gauge whether the behaviour of civil servants changed; there is evidence officials are more cautious and apprehensive than in the past (Sausman and Locke 2004: 112; Savoie 2008; Aucoin 2012). The National Audit Office (NAO) criticised perma-

[24] Interview with a former departmental permanent secretary, 6th April 2018.
[25] https://www.theguardian.com/politics/2014/oct/28/civil-service-john-manzoni-job-sabmiller Accessed 5th February 2018.
[26] Interview with a departmental permanent secretary, 19th October 2016.

nent secretaries, 'for being too responsive to the political demands of Ministers, and insufficiently attentive to their duties as accounting officers'.[27] Another observer recently concluded: 'The senior civil service's ability to offer frank advice has been cowed by the Prime Minister's detailed insistence on everything going her way'.[28]

The reluctance to offend Ministers is considerable during transitions when officials are anxious to demonstrate loyalty; they risk reverting to being 'yes men' or 'yes women' who do not provide sufficient challenge.[29] Yet the willingness to tell Ministers they are wrong is vital for decision-making; the questioning approach provided by civil servants is 'the golden thread' running through the British system of governance[30]:

> Some of my civil service friends who were in office when Labour came to power in 1997 have said: 'We bent over backwards too far to show that we weren't in the pockets of their outgoing rivals, and we should have been tougher with them'. There were insufficient caveats and 'wait a minutes'... There's always a danger of that after a long period of government by one party. But the best of them have always managed to speak truth under power without flattening the secretary of state; it's the way they do it.[31]

A National Audit Office (NAO) report on the work of the Department for Education under Gove found among civil servants, 'There is a lot of fear. Staff feel if they put their heads above the parapet they will be seen as an awkward character who could be got rid of' (Garner 2011). According to one former official:

> Gove was at war with his department...over fundamental issues of policy and what the department is for. Michael won. The Department for Education is now a different organisation to what it was in 2010. It is much more operational, much more involved in schools. The Permanent Secretary who inherited that [Jonathan Slater]...his view is that the department's policy-

[27] https://www.civilserviceworld.com/articles/opinion/nick-pearce-when-government-has-agreed-position---eu-referendum---civil-servants Accessed 6th February 2018.

[28] http://www.civilservant.org.uk/csr_detail-note18.html Accessed 12th December 2017.

[29] Interview with Whitehall Think-Tank research fellow, 12th December 2017.

[30] https://www.civilserviceworld.com/profile-peter-hennessy Accessed 15th December 2017.

[31] https://www.civilserviceworld.com/profile-peter-hennessy Accessed 15th December 2017.

making capacity, its ability to give Ministers the support they needed, had been gutted.[32]

The mark of civil service resistance was evident in, 'increased use of letters of dissent from permanent secretaries where they formally registered their disagreement with advice that the Secretary of State has overridden'.[33] By early 2013, relations between politicians and officials reached 'a new low' following the West Coast mainline 'debacle'; disputes between mandarins and their superiors were escalating (Watts 2013). 'Bob Kerslake was being briefed against massively while Francis Maude made multiple statements that were very disparaging of the civil service'.[34] Kerslake was removed from position as Head of the Civil Service; his departure was announced in July 2014 (Haddon 2016). As Home Secretary, May got into a dispute with Brodie Clark, the Head of the UK Border Agency over intelligence-led border checks; her political team responded by attempting, 'to smear a public servant of forty years standing' (Shipman 2017: 175). Gove was appointed Secretary of State at the Ministry of Justice (MoJ) in 2014. He was determined to remove officials who dissented:

> Indra Morris was literally sacked as Director-General [in the Ministry of Justice]...the policy advice was not in line [with Gove's thinking]. There was too much policy challenge coming to Michael [Gove] and he didn't like it. The department was utterly dysfunctional but at the same time a huge public policy disaster was unfolding...The prison system pretty much collapsed...policy-making was weakened and the machine was gutted.[35]

The signal to the civil service could hardly be clearer; officials who disagreed with the policy line of Ministers risked marginalisation or termination of their careers. They could not expect to be defended by the Cabinet Secretary. In DfE and MoJ, civil servants put their jobs on the line by objecting to Minister's decisions. For example, MoJ Ministers accepted a 25 per cent cut in the prison budget implying a 30 per cent decline in prison officers between 2010 and 2014, despite the fact prisoner numbers in England reached 86,000—an all-time high; in agreeing to the Treasury's

---

[32] Interview with former Treasury and Cabinet Office official, 11th January 2018.
[33] Interview with former Head of the Number Ten Policy Unit, 12th February 2012.
[34] Interview with Whitehall Think-Tank research fellow, 12th December 2017.
[35] Interview with former Treasury and Cabinet Office official, 11th January 2018.

cuts, Ministers went against the advice of officials.[36] The impact was a breakdown of trust undermining the 'governing marriage'.

CONCLUSION

The evidence is 'personalisation' of appointments grew substantially after 2010. According to NPG, Ministers pursue partisan goals creating teams of handpicked officials loyal to politicians (Savoie 2008). Britain moved closer to the Australian model. Civil service appointments are tailored to the Minister's predilections. Maude pursued, 'a performance contract model where the Permanent Secretary is held accountable'.[37] Personalisation is attractive to politicians who want civil servants around them enthusiastically defending their policies. The risk, however, is that officials are more reluctant to express views 'freely and frankly'. In Australia, an archetypal example of the Westminster tradition, 'As civil servants' tenure increasingly depends on the goodwill of the Minister, they are less likely to present unbiased and accurate advice' (Qvortrup 2005). The situation has disastrous implications for policy-making and governance.

Moreover, personalisation weakens the loyalty of officials to departments and colleagues, undermining the trust previously animating the Whitehall model. Increasingly, permanent secretaries have to work at the centre of government (Number Ten, the Cabinet Office, the Treasury) where they are 'visible' to the Prime Minister to gain promotion (Savoie 2008: 17). The problem is civil servants only learn how to run operational functions in when based in departments. When Nick Timothy and Fiona Hill were May's advisers in Number Ten, civil servants complained Jeremy Heywood and the Prime Minister's Principle Private Secretary, Simon Case, failed to protect them from the internal culture of blame-games and 'punishment-beatings'; one official said of Case: 'I felt he regularly threw a load of us under a bus'; when civil servants were being intimidated and harangued, senior managers were 'completely absent' according to another official (cited in Shipman 2017: 171). One Whitehall 'watcher' noted after May became Prime Minister, 'In a little recognised but very consequential move for how Whitehall operates, a veritable putsch was organised to get rid of all the senior officials that May disliked (essentially anyone 'speaking

---

[36] Cited in https://www.civilserviceworld.com/articles/opinion/sir-leigh-lewis-so-white-halls-fighting-back-good---civil-service-shouldnt-be Accessed 2nd February 2018.
[37] Interview with a former departmental permanent secretary, 6th April 2018.

truth to power')'.[38] Officials were 'bemused' at, 'the violation of past norms of behaviour that has already gone on under Conservative majority rule'; Case was accused of flagrant 'quiescence' in the face of 'naked politicisation'.[39]

There is evidence the demarcation between 'politics' and 'administration' was being worn away. The personalisation of appointments disheartened and unnerved mandarins; reciprocity between Ministers and officials was undermined. The IfG's conclusions are apposite:

> In recent years, tensions and mistrust at the top of Whitehall have been exposed on a frequent basis. There has been public criticism of civil servants—by Ministers and anonymous briefers—on issues such as Universal Credit, the West Coast Mainline decision, and the pace of civil service reform. There has been a relatively high turnover of permanent secretaries, which in part reflects ministerial dissatisfaction with their senior officials. There has been briefing in the other direction too, with officials (or at least ex-officials) criticising the Government's direction of reform and its treatment of the Civil Service...It does appear that amidst the turbulence of large-scale spending cuts, headcount reductions and structural reform, relationships between Ministers and senior officials are at a low point. (Paun and Harris 2013: 4)

The Whitehall model is at a turning-point. The impact of structural reforms of the civil service has been far-reaching, leading to irreversible changes in the institutions and practices of British government. The culture of the British civil service is being altered fundamentally. There will almost certainly be no return to the paradigm brokered in the last century.

BIBLIOGRAPHY

Addison, P. (1976). *The Road to 1945*. London: Quartet Books.

Agbonlahor, W. (2013, December 2). Lord Butler Criticises Churn Among Perm Secs. *Civil Service World*.

Aucoin, P. (2012). New Political Governance in Westminster Systems: Impartial Public Administration and Management Performance at Risk. *Governance, 25*(2), 177–199.

---

[38] Cited in http://www.civilservant.org.uk/csr_detail-note18.html   Accessed   12th December 2017.

[39] Cited in http://www.civilservant.org.uk/csr_detail-note18.html   Accessed   12th December 2017.

Bakvis, H., & Jarvis, M. (Eds.). (2012). Introduction: Peter C. Aucoin: From New Public Management to New Political Governance. In *From New Public Management to New Political Governance*. McGill-Queens University Press.

Beland, D., & Cox, R. H. (2011). *Ideas and Politics in Social Science Research*. Oxford: Oxford University Press.

Cannadine, D. (2017). *Victorious Century: The United Kingdom 1800–1906*. London: Allen Lane.

Freeguard, G., et al. (2015). *Whitehall Monitor 2015*. London: Institute for Government.

Garner, R. (2011, September 23). Crisis of Confidence Among Civil Servants in Gove's Department. *The Independent*.

Haddon, C. (2016). Developments in the Civil Service. In R. Heffernan, C. Hay, M. Russell, & P. Cowley (Eds.), *Developments in British Politics 10*. Basingstoke: Palgrave Macmillan.

Institute for Government (IfG). (2018). *The Whitehall Monitor 2018: The General Election, Brexit and Beyond*. London: IfG.

McClory, J. (2010, November 10). *Will 'New Style' Departmental Boards Kill or Cure?* London: Institute for Government.

Normington, D. (2013, January 16). Letter to the Times Newspaper.

O'Malley, M. (2017). Temporary Partisans, Tagged Officers or Impartial Professionals: Moving Between Ministerial Offices and Departments. *Public Administration, 95*(1), 407–420.

Paun, A., & Harris, J. (2012). *Reforming Civil Service Accountability*. London: Institute for Government.

Paun, A., & Harris, J. (2013). *Accountability at the Top: Supporting Effective Leadership in Whitehall*. London: Institute for Government.

Paun, A., et al. (2010). *Shaping Up: A Whitehall for the Future?* London: Institute for Government.

Qvortrup, M. (2005). *Memorandum to the Select Committee on Public Administration – Written Evidence*. London: House of Commons.

Sausman, C., & Locke, R. (2004). The British Civil Service: Examining the Question of Politicisation. In G. B. Peters & J. Pierre (Eds.), *Politicisation of the Civil Service in Comparative Perspective* (pp. 101–124). London: Routledge.

Savoie, D. (2008). *Court Government and the Collapse of Accountability in Canada and the United Kingdom*. Toronto: University of Toronto Press.

Shipman, T. (2017). *Fall Out: A Year of Political Mayhem*. London: William Collins.

Watts, R. (2013, February 16). Ministers' New Plan to Steamroller Civil Servants. *The Daily Telegraph*.

Wildavsky, A. (1979). *Speaking Truth to Power: The Art and Craft of Policy Analysis*. New York: Little Brown.

CHAPTER 5

A 'Promiscuously Partisan' Bureaucracy

INTRODUCTION

The cumulative effect of these changes makes the central government machine in the UK 'promiscuously partisan' (Aucoin 2012). Officials are expected to support the government's agenda. The norms of 'impartial loyalty' are displaced by partisanship (Bakvis and Jarvis 2012: 17). The civil service always counselled Ministers on the political dimensions of policy decisions; yet now, substantive advice is outweighed by partisan considerations (Van den Berg 2016). Civil servants are required to advocate government policies, persuading the media and stakeholders the government's measures are in the public interest (Aucoin 2012: 189). As the civil service 'monopoly' over policy-making is weakened, officials are compelled to demonstrate allegiance to Ministers. This chapter will consider the dramatic growth of 'promiscuous partisanship' in Whitehall.

Under New Political Governance (NPG), the bureaucratic machinery in the British state has become increasingly partisan. The advisory system is open to actors who have political links to the governing party (Craft and Halligan 2015: 2–3). More outside experts enter Whitehall. Civil servants are under pressure to demonstrate loyalty or risk irrelevance. Alongside 'promiscuous partisanship', there has been a dramatic reduction in the institutional capacities of Whitehall. Since 2010, for example, there have been major cuts in civil service numbers, while agencies are being reconfigured. The so-called 'austerity agenda' leads to greater outsourcing, as

© The Author(s) 2019
P. Diamond, *The End of Whitehall?*,
https://doi.org/10.1007/978-3-319-96101-9_5

politicians are encouraged to identify new capacities for policy implementation outside the central state.

DEFENDING GOVERNMENT POLICY

It has to be said there is nothing unusual about civil servants representing, even endorsing government policy. After all, the role of mandarins is to employ policy-making skills to advance the government's agenda (Grube 2015). Officials must negotiate the 'loyalty paradox' in Whitehall's administrative tradition. Civil servants should faithfully serve the government of the day, but not the partisan interests of the governing party (O'Malley 2017: 404; Aucoin 2012). Where to draw the line between legitimate loyalty and overt partisanship is hardly clear-cut. It is not obvious the Treasury's support for austerity since 2010 proves a shift has taken place from norms of non-partisan loyalty to 'promiscuous partisanship'. For the last century, the Treasury has advocated fiscal prudence and a 'disciplined' approach to the public finances.

Moreover, compelling the civil service to be accountable to Parliament, as Maude desired, actually makes officials *more* independent. Margaret Hodge, the former Chair of the House of Commons Public Accounts Committee (PAC), insisted civil servants should, 'unambiguously answer to Parliament'. In a 2016 speech, for example, she declared:

> The old convention of civil servants being accountable to Ministers who are accountable to parliament is broken. It worked when Haldane invented it after the First World War when there were only 28 civil servants in the Home Office. Today, despite the cuts, there are 28,000. (Cited in Civil Service World 2016)

The direct accountability of mandarins makes civil servants less liable to political control and less likely to act as 'promiscuous partisans'. Another development is 'depoliticisation', the propensity for governments to 'offload' responsibility, taking politics out of policy-making by creating independent central banks and arms-length bodies (Burnham 2002). In such circumstances, it is hard to foresee officials will become more one-sided or aligned to any particular party. Civil servants avoid cultivating a 'public face', preferring to maintain 'quiet anonymity' (Grube 2015: 305). It isn't clear any unilateral shift towards 'promiscuous partisanship' has occurred. Yet the pressure for civil servants to comply with their political masters is unmistakable.

THE PUBLIC VISIBILITY OF MANDARINS

Rod Rhodes (cited in Grube 2015: 306) observes: 'Nowadays, senior civil servants speak in public almost as often as Ministers'. The civil service is, 'far more visible', as the result of, 'parliamentary procedure, select committees being televised on camera, twitter and the Internet'.[1] The chief executives of government quangos answer to the public for mistakes which occur on their watch (Sausman and Locke 2004). Officials are more willing to articulate the government's priorities, but it is likely civil servants will be caught up in 'blame games' that result from poorly conceived policies.

The role of the Treasury and departments in the Scottish 2014 Independence referendum and the 2016 referendum on UK membership of the European Union (EU) raised questions about the insidious growth of partisanship in Whitehall. It is alleged officials over stepped the mark while, 'there is a balancing act for the civil service to play in thinking about their reputation as an independent arbiter for truth and fact'.[2] The Cameron Administration insisted it was legitimate to use the official machine to advance arguments against Scottish independence and British exit from the EU. The government of the day had, 'a clear policy position'; yet the refusal to issue 'purdah guidelines' put the civil service in an awkward and conflicted position.[3] In the Brexit referendum the decision to 're-run project fear…damaged the Treasury'.[4]

The Treasury Permanent Secretary, Nicholas Macpherson, took the unprecedented step of publishing formal advice given to the Chancellor of the Exchequer on a currency union were Scotland to have voted for independence.[5] As Peter Riddell, the former Director of the IfG remarked:

> The publication of personal advice from a permanent secretary to a Minister is highly unusual…in the midst of a major national political debate. This may be a well thought through departure from the usual rules, in which case the civil service, parliament and public need to be informed at the earliest

[1] Interview with Whitehall Think-Tank research fellow, 12th December 2017.
[2] Interview with Whitehall Think-Tank research fellow, 12th December 2017.
[3] https://www.instituteforgovernment.org.uk/blog/purdah-and-role-civil-service-eu-referendum Accessed 20th January 2018.
[4] Interview with a former departmental permanent secretary, 6th April 2018.
[5] https://www.gov.uk/government/uploads/system/uploads/attachment_data/file/279460/Sir_Nicholas_Macpherson_-_Scotland_and_a_currency_union.pdf Accessed 7th February 2018.

opportunity as to how the new system will operate. The concern is that this was a hasty decision that will have unintended consequences for advice given to Ministers on future major issues—including referendums.[6]

Macpherson went beyond the remit of the 'apolitical' civil servant, undermining the case for independence while attacking the fiscal policies of the Scottish Government.[7] The strident terms in which Macpherson's memorandum was drafted is striking:

> Currency unions between sovereign states are fraught with difficulty. They require extraordinary commitment, and a genuine desire to see closer union between the peoples involved. As the Treasury paper points out, the great thing about the sterling union between Scotland, Wales, Northern Ireland and England is that it has all the necessary ingredients: political union, economic integration and consent. What worries me about the Scottish Government's putative currency union is that it would take place against the background of a weakening union between the two countries, running counter to the direction of travel in the Eurozone. I would advise strongly against a currency union as currently advocated, if Scotland were to vote for independence.[8]

Macpherson was drawn into putting a knife through the case for independence: 'He completely tore a hole through the principle of advice being given confidentially'.[9] While officials can refuse to be drawn into partisan arguments, 'formal guidelines' contained in the Civil Service Code, 'leave little room for the civil service to resist pressure to actively justify government policy' (Grube 2015: 307). All too often, officials are forced to comply with the instructions of politicians. As one permanent secretary recounts:

> Policy-based evidence-making [in Whitehall] was endemic. We do things too quickly even if they are sensitive…the pressures on government to

---

[6] https://www.instituteforgovernment.org.uk/news/latest/ifg-statement-hm-treasury-letter-chancellor Accessed 6th February 2018.

[7] https://www.ft.com/content/fb08c6f8-e9a3-38a3-b08b-fc4528abb698 Accessed 5th February 2018.

[8] https://www.gov.uk/government/uploads/system/uploads/attachment_data/file/279460/Sir_Nicholas_Macpherson_-_Scotland_and_a_currency_union.pdf Accessed 6th February 2018.

[9] Interview with a former departmental permanent secretary, 6th April 2018.

deliver quickly are so strong. It is microwave not slow cooker government...
The civil service is becoming more transactional.[10]

Treasury officials supported the Cameron Government's austerity strategy against the advice of numerous economists. *The Financial Times* reported that since the 2008 crash, Macpherson, 'has been an enthusiastic advocate of austerity and supports George Osborne's target of an absolute surplus by 2020' (Parker 2016). Macpherson's approach was consistent with the long-standing 'Treasury view', emphasising the importance of fiscal discipline and 'sound money' to protect the UK from economic instability and capital flight (Macpherson 2013). He argued it is not the job of the civil service to be 'impartial'; officials are expected to be, 'strong champions of a policy'.[11]

However, when officials become cheerleaders for the economic and political strategy of the incumbent government, the danger is the quality of policy advice will be diminished. Critics argue the Treasury is vulnerable to 'group-think', 'the tendency to follow a standard organisational line'. There is an 'embedded departmental culture' which means the views of outsiders are seldom taken seriously; disagreements are deliberately suppressed.[12] As one official opined, 'There are deep-seated issues about how the Treasury works'.[13]

CONCLUSION

These examples support claims of 'promiscuous partisanship' in the permanent bureaucracy. The Treasury was criticised for failing to consider other approaches offering an alternative macro-economic prescription to austerity. As a result of the 'permanent campaign', Whitehall is contaminated by partisan objectives which officials are expected to endorse.

Ministers increasingly turn to figures outside government to provide an authoritative independent voice. The previous Government appointed Derek Wanless to examine NHS funding; the Cameron Administration recruited Andrew Dilnot to consider the future structure of social care.[14]

[10] Interview with a departmental permanent secretary, 19th October 2016.
[11] Interview with Whitehall Think-Tank research fellow, 12th December 2017.
[12] http://www.industry-forum.org/wp-content/uploads/2017/03/9076_17-Kerslake-Review-of-the-Treasury-_-final_v2.pdf Accessed 22nd January 2018.
[13] Interview with a former departmental permanent secretary, 6th April 2018.
[14] Interview with Whitehall Think-Tank research fellow, 12th December 2017.

The reputation of the civil service in providing untarnished, objective analysis has been diminished. Officials are no longer regarded as unimpeachable, trusted advisers. The British system of government and the quality of the policy-making process is weaker as a consequence.

BIBLIOGRAPHY

Aucoin, P. (2012). New Political Governance in Westminster Systems: Impartial Public Administration and Management Performance at Risk. *Governance, 25*(2), 177–199.

Bakvis, H., & Jarvis, M. (Eds.). (2012). Introduction: Peter C. Aucoin: From New Public Management to New Political Governance. In *From New Public Management to New Political Governance*. McGill-Queens University Press.

Burnham, P. (2002). New Labour and the Politics of Depoliticisation. *British Journal of Politics and International Relations, 3*(2), 127–149.

Civil Service World. (2016, March 4). Margaret Hodge: Accountability System for Civil Servants Is 'Broken' – But MPs Are More Interested in New Policies Than Value for Money.

Craft, J., & Halligan, J. (2015, July 1–4). *Looking Back and Thinking Ahead: 30 Years of Policy Advisory System Scholarship.* Prepared for T08P06 Comparing Policy Advisory Systems. International Conference on Public Policy. Catholic University of Sacro Cuore, Milan.

Grube, D. (2015). Responsibility to Be Enthusiastic? Public Servants and the Public Face of 'Promiscuous Partisanship'. *Governance, 28*(3), 305–320.

Macpherson, N. (2013, January 16). Speech by the Permanent Secretary to the Treasury, Sir Nicholas Macpherson: The Origins of Treasury Control. https://www.gov.uk/government/speeches/speech-by-the-permanent-secretary-to-the-treasury-sir-nicholas-macpherson-the-origins-of-treasury-control

O'Malley, M. (2017). Temporary Partisans, Tagged Officers or Impartial Professionals: Moving Between Ministerial Offices and Departments. *Public Administration, 95*(1), 407–420.

Parker, G. (2016, April 13). Veteran of Treasury Battles Tots up a Decade's Wins and Losses. *The Financial Times.*

Sausman, C., & Locke, R. (2004). The British Civil Service: Examining the Question of Politicisation. In G. B. Peters & J. Pierre (Eds.), *Politicisation of the Civil Service in Comparative Perspective* (pp. 101–124). London: Routledge.

Van den Berg, C. (2016). Dynamics in the Dutch Policy Advisory System: Externalisation, Politicisation and the Legacy of Pillarisation. *Policy Sciences, 50*(1), 63–84.

CHAPTER 6

Conclusion

INTRODUCTION

Mandarins in Britain are no longer esteemed policy advisers upholding the values of public service, but managers of contracts beholden to the neoliberal state. The civil service is transformed from 'guardians of the public realm' to 'agents of the market state' (Marquand 2014: 112). It would be a struggle to claim today's state bureaucracy is, 'pervaded by a tone of impartial public-spiritedness' (Cannadine 2017: 296). Throughout the book, two key arguments were made about the bureaucratic machinery. The first is a review of the evidence supports the claim Whitehall has drastically changed since the 1980s and 1990s. The paradigm is unrecognisable compared to fifty or one hundred years ago. The system of public administration is shaped by the ethos of the 'permanent campaign' and the New Political Governance (NPG). In the British administrative tradition, civil servants were loyal to the government of the day, not the political party comprising the government. That convention has been turned on its head. Now, officials are beholden to the governing party's agenda and its partisan motives.

The second point relates to the consequences in undermining the Whitehall paradigm which has been detrimental to the quality of statecraft. The institutions of the British state operate according to the imperatives of the 'permanent campaign' and NPG. The motivation of advisers and appointees in Whitehall is partisan, focused on loyalty to the Minister. Ministerial interference in the appointment of civil servants undermines Northcote-Trevelyan. Officials are required to implement policies they

© The Author(s) 2019
P. Diamond, *The End of Whitehall?*,
https://doi.org/10.1007/978-3-319-96101-9_6

played little or no role in formulating. Those who raise their heads above the parapet risk being ostracised. The UK's government machinery is more vulnerable than ever to 'group think' and 'promiscuous partisanship'. The Whitehall model is dissipating. Aucoin's work on NPG alerts us to the far-reaching nature of change. The concept of NPG is a major contribution to the comparative literature on public administration in the Anglophone states.

Of course, institutional change is never all encompassing. There is a risk of underestimating the resilience of the Whitehall paradigm given the relationship between Ministers and officials. There are Whitehall watchers who maintain whatever the strains in governance, the 'public service bargain' (Hood 2001) or 'governing marriage' that entrenched mutual dependency between politicians and civil servants endures (Page 2010; Burnham and Pyper 2008). The loyalty of Ministers to officials held back the tide of politicisation. Yes, there has been transformation elsewhere. After 2010, for instance, the UK became among the largest public sector outsourcing markets in the world (Smith and Jones 2015). However, trust between Ministers and officials emerged unscathed after decades of reform. Ultimately, politicians were not prepared to follow-through on plans to restructure the bureaucracy. As Hood (2007: 12) acerbically remarks:

> We have seen this movie before—albeit with a slightly different plotline— with a rash of attempts to fix up the bureaucracy, with the same pattern of hype from the centre, selective filtering at the extremities and political attention deficit syndrome that works against any follow through and continuity.

According to this perspective, the Whitehall model broadly survived; Ministers facing numerous competing pressures did not want to get involved in the hard grind of administrative reform. The ideas they battled to implement in transforming the bureaucracy were invariably confused and contradictory.

RESISTANCE TO NPG

It can thus be claimed that NPG's influence was limited. 'Veto points' include the commitment to impartiality and non-partisanship, reinforced by historic ties between officials and Ministers. Bureaucrats are adept at resisting change. The civil service contest initiatives that imperil the values of meritocracy and public service. Aucoin's work under-values the importance of 'institutionalised structures' and 'formal rules' in the Civil Service Code that restrict the ability of political actors to impose their ideas, enforcing limits on official compliance with Ministers' instructions (Grube 2015: 312). Civil servants should be understood as purposeful actors, as shrewd and calculating as their political masters: 'Nobody really believes that senior civil servants are faceless, pliable, sexless creatures without fixed ideas, or intellectual eunuchs impartially proffering advice with all deference and humility to the great man in the Minister's office' (Chapman 1964: 184).

The Cameron governments struggled to sustain momentum for administrative reform. While the Prime Minister grew frustrated by institutional obfuscation and complained about the 'buggeration factor' in getting policy through the machine, he chose not to shake up Whitehall (Theakston 2015).[1] Cameron acknowledged Ministers need support and work closely with civil servants; officials know the 'small p' politics of Whitehall's byzantine decision-making structures. Civil servants are, 'trusted advisers and partners of their Minister'.[2] *The Economist* noted when the Prime Minister came to office he espoused confidence in officials: 'His faith was that of an English patrician; Mr Cameron is drawn from the same social circles that have traditionally produced senior mandarins. There was an implicit trust'.[3] Ministers could rarely afford for confidence to break down. One observer of the Blair governments concluded: 'Labour was more deferential to the civil service than the Tories had been in 1979'.[4] The Prime Minister, 'Thought [Whitehall] was a wonderful machine...the national civil service was a dream of Rolls-Royce efficiency, full of very clever people eager to serve you'.

Cameron was, 'uninterested in reform of structures and systems'; Steve Hilton failed to persuade the Prime Minister of their importance.[5] Maude was a 'true believer' but his instincts were unusual. Maude thought like a management consultant. Like previous premiers, when civil service reform was mentioned, '[Cameron's] eyes tended to glaze over' (D'Ancona

---

[1] https://www.ft.com/content/e3424d06-c8a0-11e4-8617-00144feab7de   Accessed 22nd January 2018.

[2] Interview with a former departmental permanent secretary, 6th April 2018.

[3] https://www.economist.com/blogs/blighty/2011/03/david_cameron_versus_civil_service Accessed 18th December 2017.

[4] Interview with former Head of the Number Ten Policy Unit, 17th February 2011.

[5] Interview with former Head of the Cabinet Office Strategy Unit (PMSU), 17th February 2012.

2014). Dominic Cummings, Michael Gove's adviser, despaired at the Prime Minister's insouciance:

> Senior people [in Number Ten] issue airy instructions (usually in response to a column rather than as part of a serious plan) but...do not know how to follow things through and ensure things get done. By the time [Number Ten] realises its instructions have been ignored, months can pass.[6]

The Prime Minister lacked the 'reforming zeal' to overhaul the machine; he was unwilling to take on, 'the bureaucratic forces that militated against significant policy change' (Ashcroft and Oakeshott 2016: 378–384).

The Erosion of the Whitehall Model

Yet while Cameron was unquestionably reticent about picking fights, all recent governments have been complicit in the denigration of the Whitehall model. Aucoin was right: there have been major changes in the state bureaucracy, the consequence of a long-term transformation in the relationship between politicians and bureaucrats. Institutions have been recast in the name of new approaches to public management. Civil servants are no longer expected to highlight difficulties or point out that there are alternative ways of addressing problems; their role is to justify what politicians already decided to do, 'rigorously' implementing Ministers' ideas (Leys 2006). The commitment of civil servants and Ministers to a shared view of the state as advancing the public good has withered. The shrinking of UK government after a decade of austerity has been a further driver of change.

Whitehall Cutbacks

The Conservative-led governments after 2010 maintained, 'The era of big government has come to an end not just because the money has literally run out, but it is also shown to have failed'.[7] Tory politicians averred 'the gentleman in Whitehall' did not always 'know best'; governments had a

---

[6]Cited in Richard Garner, 'Ex-Gove Adviser Resumes Attack on Cameron', *The Independent*, 20th June 2014: http://www.independent.co.uk/news/education/education-news/michael-gove-aide-faces-questions-after-implying-journalist-needed-therapy-8503951.html Accessed 22nd November 2017.

[7]https://www.civilserviceworld.com/articles/news/cabinet-office-minister-francis-maude-you-dont-need-be-mp-do-my-job Accessed 22nd November 2017.

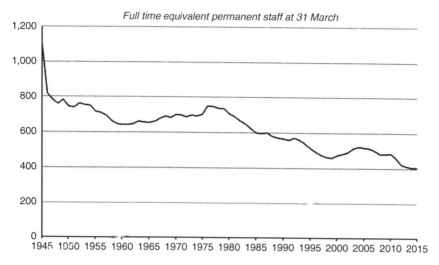

Fig. 6.1 Estimated civil service staff numbers 1945–2015 (Source: House of Lords Library, 2016)

poor record of addressing intractable problems (Norman and Ganesh 2006). The Chancellor of the Exchequer, George Osborne, set a target of eliminating the public sector deficit by 2018–2019. The deficit reduction plan required departments to make 34 per cent cuts.

The dramatic reduction in civil service numbers and the size of departments followed. As the graph below illustrates, civil service numbers declined sharply. By 2015, there were approximately 385,000 civil servants, down from 475,000 in 2010—a cumulative decline of 19 per cent; the UK civil service is smaller than at any point since the Second World War; the number of Non-Departmental Public Bodies (NDPBs) has fallen from 680 to 401 after the promised 'bonfire of the quangos' (Freeguard et al. 2017).[8] The cuts involved 'strategic reprioritisation' (Pollit 2010: 21). The Department for International Development (DFID) was protected, for example, while the Department of Communities and Local Government (DCLG) shrunk dramatically (Fig. 6.1).

The stripped down civil service changed the nature of Whitehall. On average, officials are older and concentrated in senior grades; 40 per cent

[8] https://www.ons.gov.uk/employmentandlabourmarket/peopleinwork/publicsector-personnel/bulletins/civilservicestatistics/2016#background-notes.

of civil servants are over 50, while the proportion of senior posts rose from 7 to 9 per cent; administrative staff declined from 47 to 40 per cent of the workforce, underlining the impact of automation and ICT (Freeguard et al. 2015: 62). Civil service pay was frozen and pensions became less generous.[9] 53 per cent of civil servants in the UK are women, although they occupy only 40.4 per cent of the top and middle management positions.[10]

Further changes occurred in the nature of the work civil servants do; DIFD and DWP, for example, witnessed reductions in policy jobs and an increase in 'operational delivery' roles (Freeguard et al. 2015: 65–68). Officials were more involved in managing public sector contracts and commissioning services. At the Department for Education (DfE), resources passed directly from civil servants to academy schools; the Ministry of Justice (MOJ) oversaw the 'quasi-market' in probation services but no longer directly managed providers; healthcare was delivered through an intermediate agency, NHS England, rather than the Department for Health (DOH) (Freeguard et al. 2015: 65–68). Civil servants had to upgrade procurement skills, managing increasingly complex public service markets fraught with risk (Haddon 2016). Meanwhile, the shrinkage of head-count and the dramatic squeeze on operating budgets undermined Ministers' desire to rebuild capacity at the centre of the state.

THE END OF WHITEHALL

Aucoin's work on NPG is invaluable in confronting the assumptions of historical institutionalism that have shaped the political science literature on reform and the British civil service (Page 2010; Halligan 2010; Burnham and Pyper 2008). The core problem of historical institutionalism is that it typically overstates the role of institutions and underplays the role of ideas. There is a belief that current patterns will persist indefinitely. Prevailing institutional arrangements are hard-wired into the state's structure (Guy-Peters et al. 2005). Historical institutionalists focus on embedded rules and norms. They maintain that rules and norms militate against institutional change, reinforcing path dependency. Institutions change

[9] https://www.civilservant.org.uk/information-pay-general.html Accessed 12th March 2018.
[10] https://www.google.co.uk/?client=safari&channel=ipad_bm&gws_rd=cr&dcr=0&ei=xFiqWr2OLoifgAahh4iwDA Accessed 14th March 2018.

slowly and incrementally. Yet the experience of the Whitehall model dem onstrates that is not always the case—even in a political system as adaptive as Britain's. The Whitehall paradigm is undermined as the political context has changed profoundly:

> The British picture is a complex one, best characterised as a state responding to increasingly demanding politicians while attempting to adapt to a changing social and political environment which includes a consumerist electorate and scrutinising media. (Sausman and Locke 2004: 101)

New generations of Ministers emerged sensitive to electoral imperatives; the roles of institutions and actors have been altered—civil servants have gone from being 'policy advisers' to 'managers'; exogenous changes, notably reductions in the size of the state, have compelled the civil service to adapt (Guy-Peters et al. 2005: 1285; Thelen and Steinmo 1992). The Whitehall model has been undermined not merely because of institutional change and novel management practices. The presence of alternative reform ideas, notably recurrent faith in the doctrine of 'private sector good, public sector bad', makes it possible to radically restructure Whitehall; previous ideas centred on traditional bureaucracies were believed to have failed (Guy-Peters et al. 2005). It remains the case that, 'ideas are the foundations of institutions' (Beland and Cox 2011: 9).

Whitehall has changed drastically since the 1980s. The civil service has been in a state of permanent revolution. The conclusions of the Organisation for Economic Co-operation and Development (OECD) are apposite. A dramatic, 'weakening of the policy advice function' has occurred in government departments; meanwhile, the 'ethical base' of the civil service has been aggressively attacked by importing private sector practices into central government.[11]

The Quality of Governance in Britain

The undermining of the Whitehall model is detrimental to good government. A report on the Treasury's role in the financial crisis by the Second Permanent Secretary, Sharon White, underlined the risks posed by cuts and restructuring.[12] The 'fiasco' over the West Coast mainline, where the

[11] https://www.google.co.uk/?client=safari&channel=ipad_bm&gws_rd=cr&dcr=0&ei=xFiqWr2OLoifgAahh4iwDA Accessed 11th March 2018.

[12] https://www.gov.uk/government/uploads/system/uploads/attachment_data/file/220506/review_fincrisis_response_290312.pdf Accessed 19th December 2016.

franchise tendering process was cancelled following a successful legal challenge by the train operating companies, exposed major problems. As the Laidlaw report (2012: 62) noted:

> The previous 'Rail' Director-General, the Policy Director, the Rail Service Delivery Director and the Procurement Director all retired in December 2010 and only the Policy Director and the Rail Service Delivery Director were replaced, resulting in a loss of both 'corporate memory' and individual commercial experience. In implementing substantial cost savings...the DfT significantly reduced its headcount, the number of contractors used and its use of external consultants...organisational restructuring at the DfT resulted in a lack of clarity in roles and responsibilities and in associated accountabilities...These deficiencies adversely impacted the DfT's effectiveness in identifying and/or resolving flaws in the franchise process. (2012: 64)

The Laidlaw report emphasised concerns raised in the 'first wave' of governance literature during the 1990s about the erosion of state capacity and the 'hollowing-out' of the public sector (Rhodes 1994). The link between fiscal austerity and public sector management reform is not clearcut; while an air of crisis provides the impetus for structural change, cutbacks make it hard to 'lubricate' the reform process with additional resources (Pollit 2010). Less money does not always mean major reforms.

The paradox of Maude's programme was Ministers sought to intensify political control over the bureaucratic machinery, while encouraging a more disaggregated approach to policy-making and implementation. The emphasis on contestability and outsourcing of delivery undermined the vertical authority and influence of Ministers. Oliver Letwin complained 'subject specialists' in the civil service had been side-lined in favour of management experts.[13] Ministers who made policy were increasingly detached from 'managers' and 'street-level bureaucrats'. The divergence began in the late 1980s as 'arms-length' *Next Steps* agencies were separated from departments. The Public Administration Select Committee (PASC) warned of a, 'further fracture between policy generation and delivery'.[14] Forty years of research drawing on countless implementation case-studies reinforced the point: 'policy design and implementation cannot and should not be separated' (Norris et al. 2014: 12). Yet in the British administrative tradition, they have been pulled apart almost relentlessly.

[13] https://publications.parliament.uk/pa/cm201617/cmselect/cmpubadm/253/253. pdf Accessed 2nd February 2018.
[14] https://publications.parliament.uk/pa/cm201617/cmselect/cmpubadm/253/253. pdf Accessed 2nd February 2018.

WHITEHALL: A PUBLIC SERVICE UNDER THREAT?

The evidence makes it necessary to dispute the IfG's claim that, 'the day to day business of government looks much the same' as it did twenty or thirty years ago (Freeguard et al. 2015: 5). Not only have there been major changes in the state bureaucracy. 'In Anglo-American democracies in particular, career public servants [have been] subject to an assault by politicians that was unprecedented in this century (Aucoin 1995: 113; cited in Peters and Savoie 2012: 31). May's former Chief of Staff in Number Ten, Nick Timothy was said to be deliberately, 'rude to officials and civil servants, to show that he doesn't give a f***. He did it to show he was the big boy' (cited in Shipman 2017: 157). The Communications Chief, Fiona Hill, sent abusive messages to officials as a matter of course. Hill expressed her displeasure without restraint. She once wrote: 'It is a f****** catastrophe you work for the civil service'; 'how the f*** do you work here?' (cited in Shipman 2017: 157–158).

As a consequence, 'The senior ranks of the civil service were massively demoralised…You were taking a cadre of people who were crucial to running the country and turning them into functionaries'.[15] Colin Kidd (2018: 17) wrote that during May's premiership, 'The Blairite informality of shirtsleeve, sofa government gave way to…decision making in the closet by over-mighty court favourites who seemed to control a less confident ruler'.

In Britain, civil servants are expected to do exactly what the Prime Minister and secretaries of state demand (Savoie 2008: 337). Political advisers and aides permeate Whitehall where partisan imperatives now prevail. When Ministers take exception to advice, they establish 'independent' commissions of experts who feed in *ad hoc* opinions. On issues likely to affect the governing party's electoral reputation, the centre ruthlessly enforces 'message control'. Civil servants depend on a favourable reputation among politicians to gain promotion. They are expected to enthusiastically support initiatives and carry out the orders of their political masters with conviction. The public service ethic encapsulated in the doctrines of Northcote-Trevelyan and Haldane has been worn away. Weber's distinction between 'administration' and 'politics' no longer holds true in British governance. The UK state bureaucracy has gone beyond a 'tipping-point'.

---

[15] Interview with former Treasury and Cabinet Office official, 11th January 2018.

Why, then, has the Whitehall model been replaced by NPG? The first factor is arguably the most benign. The growth of NPG relates to the legitimate desire of Ministers to utilise new streams of policy knowledge and expertise unavailable within the traditional bureaucracy. The shift is consistent with the move towards 'evidence-based' policy-making (Davies et al. 2000). Recent governments have been prepared to invest in 'evidence institutions' from agencies such as the National Institute for Health and Care Excellence (NICE) to 'what works' centres. External appointees helped to infuse the policy-making process with fresh ideas, drawing on best practice from other countries while harnessing social science research. The problem, however, is politicisation inevitably undermines evidence-led approaches.

The second factor weakening the Whitehall paradigm relates to ministerial dissatisfaction. The Whitehall model has been eroded because Ministers are less enamoured of the support they receive. Officials are perceived as obstructive or risk-averse. Their commissioning skills are roundly criticised. Civil servants are regarded as poor at managing major projects. Public trust in officials is declining.[16] As a consequence, politicians are less committed to the public service bargain. The professionalization of politics foreseen by Weber leads Ministers to require capabilities not provided by the traditional Whitehall machinery, ostracising the civil service.

The third point about the breakdown of the Whitehall model is that the NPM reforms of the 1980s and 1990s became entrenched, while the 'principal-agent' relationship where bureaucrats obey the instructions of their political masters became the norm. The spirit of NPM lives on but is augmented by the emphasis of NPG on Ministers gaining political control over policy-making. Administrative reform has continued as the result of ongoing pressures for change and improvement (Pollit 2010). Greater use of the private sector persists (Pollit 2010: 23). In the aftermath of the 2008 crisis, commentators refer to this phenomenon as 'the strange non-death of neo-liberalism' (Crouch 2011).

The fourth reason why NPG replaced the Whitehall model is the capacities of central government have been depleted; meanwhile, there is growing demand for innovation to deliver 'more for less'. The situation compels Ministers to look outside the bureaucracy for insight and implementation capacity. As a consequence, 'cosy triangles' of elite decision-making are

---

[16] https://www.civilserviceworld.com/articles/news/public-confidence-civil-servants-drops-poll-finds-%E2%80%93-theyre-still-more-trusted Accessed 12th February 2018.

replaced by 'big sloppy hexagons' of actors from across the public, private, and civil society sectors. Increasingly, management consultants and think-tanks fill the void.

The final, and most fundamental, explanation relates to the role of ideas. Both of the major political parties in Britain over the last thirty years have modified their view of the role of the state. The Conservative party has become more ideological and since the 1970s, increasingly hostile to the collectivism of British government. Conservative politicians were receptive to ideas developed in the United States that influenced the 'Reagan revolution' which sought to curtail the size, power and legitimacy of public bureaucracies in the name of the neo-liberal 'market state'. The rise of 'ideas-driven' Conservatism meant the Tory party became 'addicted' to abstract ideas about how to remake the state in the name of free market principles.[17] The UK thus became one of the leaders in the enactment of the NPM paradigm. The growing prominence of economics and the institutionalisation of economic knowledge within British government were a further spur to the promulgation of rational choice and NPM ideas (Christensen 2014: 161).

The Labour party too became increasingly dissatisfied with the state by the end of the twentieth century. For much of the previous hundred years, Labour politicians assumed the British constitution and the system of government enabled the smooth implementation of a socialist programme. The 1945 Attlee Government affirmed the amenability of British governing institutions to the Left. Yet by the late 1990s, New Labour saw the state as antiquated, in need of urgent modernisation. There was growing receptivity to NPM ideas, and in due course, to the principal prescriptions of NPG. Labour Ministers sought greater leverage over the policy-making process. Structural reforms of public service organisations, the creation of new government units, and the recruitment of additional staff into Whitehall led to ideational change (Christensen 2014: 177). Blair's Labour party was wedded to the ethos of the 'permanent campaign', managing Whitehall accordingly.

The evidence indicates all the key Anglophone countries experienced conflict between politicians and administrators in recent decades. The basic precepts of the Weberian model that 'politics' and 'administration' are separate domains with their own ethos and rationale was undermined. The motives of

---

[17] https://www.lrb.co.uk/v39/n23/jonathan-parry/whats-the-big-idea Accessed 27th February 2018.

political actors in recasting governance institutions are not always ill-intentioned. NPG arises as governors across the western world wrestle with a host of problems from the challenges of managing the mass media to demands for greater transparency and openness. The 'platonic ideal' of the Whitehall model has been undermined by factors that go beyond the remit or intensions of individual politicians, notably the changing role of the state, the professionalization of politics, the growth of a virulent strain of 'anti-politics', and the rise of the new media.[18]

NPG diverges from prior concepts of 'governance' emphasising the dispersal of authority and the fragmentation of state capacity. An increasingly complex administrative landscape marked by the erosion of vertical hierarchies led Ministers to rebuild capacity and control at the centre of the state (Peters 2005). Fragmentation was as fundamental for the civil service as politicisation; the growth of agencies and public bodies depleted the cohesion and *esprit de corps* of Whitehall, undermining the drive towards joined-up government.[19] The weakness of the literature on the 'hollowing-out' of government and 'the differentiated polity' is the claim traditional power relationships were dissolving as influence shifted 'upwards' to the European Union (EU), 'downwards' to local agencies, and 'sideways' to the private sector (Rhodes 1997; Bevir and Rhodes 2003). In fact, numerous Whitehall hierarchies and power structures remained, but were adapted by politicians to suit the imperatives of the NPG-style 'permanent campaign'.

CONCLUSION: NPG AND THE BRITISH CONSTITUTION

The replacement of the Whitehall model by NPG machinery has far-reaching consequences that ought to be thoroughly debated across the public sphere. Legitimate questions have arisen about how far the actions of political advisers can be scrutinised? Should the appointment of advisers be regulated by an independent body? To what extent can civil servants be protected from political interference, helping governments avoid 'policy blunders'? What role should Ministers play in the appointment of permanent secretaries? These are fundamental questions that deserve to be aired in any debate about the future of Britain and its governing institutions. It won't be pos-

---

[18] Interview with Whitehall Think-Tank research fellow, 12th December 2017.
[19] https://www.theguardian.com/politics/2002/apr/09/Whitehall.uk Accessed 19th December 2017.

sible to return to a 'golden age' where the traditional Whitehall paradigm is resurrected. Answers for the next fifty years are unlikely to be found in the orthodoxies of Northcote-Trevelyan or Haldane, however revered.

Repairing British governance is not only to do with restoring constitutional propriety and basic principles of accountability. The central issue is about what the state has the capacity to do and how the system of government is organised to deal with the most pressing social and economic problems of our time. 'Neo-Weberians' criticise NPM reforms, claiming societies need 'strong states' to address major challenges: to ensure the resilience of financial systems, deal with internal political conflicts, manage diversity and multiculturalism, and respond to the wave of demographic and environmental sustainability pressures (Dunn and Miller 2007). 'Innovation societies' require 'competent' public administration capable of thinking for the long-term (Bouckaert and Mikeladze 2008).

Bouckaert (2017) maintains that states are vital for managing 'wicked' policy issues, while representative democracy is essential for maintaining legitimacy.[20] The growth of digital government points the way towards innovative delivery techniques creating a new generation of 'user-led' provision.[21] But there is no reason why traditional public service virtues ought to be cast aside. The civil service has to rediscover its role as an independent arbiter, a source of authoritative judgement in an era of 'post-truth' democracy. When the Blair Government came to office, its instinct was to modernise political communications to articulate the central message of the Administration. Over the last twenty years, however, the state bureaucracy has been contaminated by the rise of the 'spin' machine and the imperatives of the 'permanent campaign'. Democratic institutions have been hollowed-out. The autonomy and independence of civil servants has been undermined.

We are witnessing, 'a general crisis of authority' as well as growing tension between 'generalism' and 'expertise' that is troubling (Kidd and Rose 2017: 251). There are more 'policy fiascos' and 'blunders' as policy-making and implementation move in separate directions. As King attests, 'part of the problem is the sheer velocity with which most Ministers evidently feel compelled to act...the spectacle resembles a nineteenth century

---

[20] 'Wicked' policy problems are inherently complex and cut across conventional institutional boundaries.

[21] http://mikebracken.com/blog/on-policy-and-delivery/ Accessed 15th December 2017.

cavalry charge'.[22] The rational Weberian model is under attack from the 'entrepreneurs of the state'—think-tanks, management consultants, unelected advisers—who stalk Whitehall at Ministers' behest. There are sources of territorial division and structural divergence arising from the growth of nationalist sentiment in Wales, Scotland and England, as well as disputes surrounding Britain's decision to leave the EU in June 2016.

Moreover, there has been a dramatic erosion of trust in the civil service underlined by the unseemly, tactless interventions of the bureaucracy in the 2014 and 2016 referendums. Officials must never be supplicants, blindly following the edicts of their political masters. They must not be afraid to think for themselves, and they must demonstrate mandarins have minds of their own.[23] Civil servants have a vital role to play in safeguarding the institutions of British democracy and the integrity of public policy, upholding the separation of powers essential for a well-governed state.

POSTSCRIPT: BREXIT

Britain's decision to leave the EU in 2016 has seismic implications for the machinery of government. Further change in Whitehall resulting from diplomatic and regulatory divergence from Europe is inevitable. The view Whitehall has been fundamentally altered is likely to be strengthened in the coming decades. It may be that cuts in the size of the bureaucracy are reversed after Brexit. What cannot easily be undone is the loss of policy-making capability and institutional memory in Whitehall, raising fundamental questions about the British state's capacity to steer a sensible course through the perilous post-Brexit landscape.

BIBLIOGRAPHY

Ashcroft, M., & Oakeshott, I. (2016). *Call Me Dave: The Unauthorised Biography of David Cameron*. Oxford: Blackwell.
Aucoin, P. (1995). *The New Public Management: Canada in Comparative Perspective*. Montreal: Institute for Research and Public Policy.
Beland, D., & Cox, R. H. (2011). *Ideas and Politics in Social Science Research*. Oxford: Oxford University Press.

[22] Cited in http://www.civilservant.org.uk/index.html#reform Accessed 2nd February 2018.
[23] https://www.lrb.co.uk/v02/n16/david-marquand/lessons-for-civil-servants Accessed 15th February 2018.

Bevir, M., & Rhodes, R. (2003). *Interpreting British Governance*. London: Routledge.

Bouckaert, G. (2017). Taking Stock of 'Governance': A Predominantly European Perspective. *Governance, 30*(1), 45–52.

Bouckaert, G., & Mikeladze, M. (2008). Introduction. *NISPAee Journal of Public Administration, 1*(2), 7–8.

Burnham, P., & Pyper, J. (2008). *Britain's Modernised Civil Service*. Basingstoke: Palgrave Macmillan.

Cannadine, D. (2017). *Victorious Century: The United Kingdom 1800–1906*. London: Allen Lane.

Chapman, B. (1964). British Government Observed. *Public Administration, 42*(2), 184–185.

Christensen, J. (2014). *The Power of Economists Within the State*. Stanford: Stanford University Press.

Crouch, C. (2011). *The Strange Non-Death of Neo-Liberalism*. Cambridge: Polity Press.

D'Ancona, M. (2014). *In It Together: The Inside Story of a Coalition Government*. London: Viking.

Davies, H. T. O., Nutley, S. M., & Smith, P. C. (2000). Introducing Evidence-Based Policy and Practice in Public Services. In H. T. O. Davies, S. M. Nutley, & P. C. Smith (Eds.), *What Works? Evidence-Based Policy and Practice in Public Services*. Bristol: Policy Press.

Dunn, W. M., & Miller, D. Y. (2007). A Critique of the New Public Management and the Neo-Weberian State: Advancing a Critical Theory of Administrative Reform. *Public Organization Review, 7*(1), 345–358.

Freeguard, G., et al. (2015). *Whitehall Monitor 2015*. London: Institute for Government.

Freeguard, G., et al. (2017). *Whitehall Monitor 2017*. London: Institute for Government.

Grube, D. (2015). Responsibility to Be Enthusiastic? Public Servants and the Public Face of 'Promiscuous Partisanship'. *Governance, 28*(3), 305–320.

Guy-Peters, B. G., King, D., & Pierre, J. (2005). The Politics of Path Dependency: Political Conflict in Historical Institutionalism. *The Journal of Politics, 67*(4), 1275–1300.

Haddon, C. (2016). Developments in the Civil Service. In R. Heffernan, C. Hay, M. Russell, & P. Cowley (Eds.), *Developments in British Politics 10*. Basingstoke: Palgrave Macmillan.

Halligan, J. (2010). The Fate of Administrative Tradition in Anglophone Countries During the Reform Era. In M. Painter & B. G. Guy-Peters (Eds.), *Tradition and Public Administration*. Basingstoke: Palgrave Macmillan.

Hood, C. (2001). *Public Service Bargains and Public Service Reform*. In B. G. Peters & J. Pierre (Eds.), *Politicians, Bureaucrats and Administrative Reform, Routledge/ECPR Studies in European Political Science* (pp. 13–23). London: Routledge.

Hood, C. (2007). What Happens When Transparency Meets Blame Avoidance. *Public Management Review, 9*(2), 191–210.

Independent Report of the Laidlaw Inquiry. (2012). *Inquiry into the Lessons Learned for the Department for Transport from the InterCity West Coast Competition.* HMG: Department of Transport.

Kidd, C. (2018, January 25). You Know Who You Are. *The London Review of Books.*

Kidd, C., & Rose, J. (2017). The Perils of Policy Advice. *Juncture, 23*(4), 242–253.

Leys, C. (2006). The Cynical State. In *The Socialist Register.* London: Merlin Press.

Marquand, D. (2014). *Mammon's Kingdom: An Essay on Britain, Now.* London: Allen Lane.

Norman, J., & Ganesh, J. (2006). *Compassionate Conservatism: What It Is and Why We Need It.* London: Policy Exchange.

Norris, E., Kidson, M., Bouchal, P., & Rutter, J. (2014). *Doing Them Justice: Lessons from Four Cases of Policy Implementation.* London: Institute for Government/Joseph Rowntree Foundation.

Page, E. (2010). Has the Whitehall Model Survived? *International Journal of Administrative Sciences, 76*(3), 407–423.

Peters, B. G. (2005). The Problem of Policy Problems. *Journal of Comparative Policy Analysis: Research and Practice, 7*(4), 349–370.

Peters, G.-P., & Savoie, D. (2012). In Search of Good Governance. In H. Bakvis & M. Jarvis (Eds.), *From New Public Management to New Political Governance* (pp. 29–45). McGill-Queens University Press.

Pollit, C. (2010). Cuts and Reforms – Public Services as We Move into a New Era. *Society and Economy, 32*(1), 17–31.

Rhodes, R. A. W. (1994). The Hollowing Out of the State: The Changing Nature of the Public Service in Britain. *The Political Quarterly, 65*(2), 138–151.

Rhodes, R. A. W. (1997). *Understanding Governance: Policy Networks, Governance, Reflexivity and Accountability.* Philadelphia, PA: Open University Press.

Sausman, C., & Locke, R. (2004). The British Civil Service: Examining the Question of Politicisation. In G. B. Peters & J. Pierre (Eds.), *Politicisation of the Civil Service in Comparative Perspective* (pp. 101–124). London: Routledge.

Savoie, D. (2008). *Court Government and the Collapse of Accountability in Canada and the United Kingdom.* Toronto: University of Toronto Press.

Shipman, T. (2017). *Fall Out: A Year of Political Mayhem.* London: William Collins.

Smith, M. J., & Jones, R. (2015). From Big Society to Small State: Conservatism and the Privatisation of Government. *British Politics, 10*(2), 226–248.

Theakston, K. (2015). David Cameron as Prime Minister. *British Politics Review, 10*(2), 6–7.

Thelen, K., & Steinmo, S. (1992). Historical Institutionalism in Comparative Politics. In S. Steinmo, K. Thelen, & F. Longstreth (Eds.), *Structuring Politics: Historical Institutionalism in Comparative Analysis.* Cambridge: Cambridge University Press.

BIBLIOGRAPHY

Addison, P. (1976). *The Road to 1945*. London: Quartet Books.

Agbonlahor, W. (2013, December 2). Lord Butler Criticises Churn Among Perm Secs. *Civil Service World*.

Ashcroft, M., & Oakeshott, I. (2016). *Call Me Dave: The Unauthorised Biography of David Cameron*. Oxford: Blackwell.

Attlee, C. A. R. (1956). Civil Servants, Ministers, Parliament and the Public. In W. Robson (Ed.), *The Civil Service in Britain and France*. London: Steven & Sons.

Aucoin, P. (1995). *The New Public Management: Canada in Comparative Perspective*. Montreal: Institute for Research and Public Policy.

Aucoin, P. (2012). New Political Governance in Westminster Systems: Impartial Public Administration and Management Performance at Risk. *Governance, 25*(2), 177–199.

Bakvis, H., & Jarvis, M. (Eds.). (2012). Introduction: Peter C. Aucoin: From New Public Management to New Political Governance. In *From New Public Management to New Political Governance*. McGill-Queens University Press.

Bale, T. (2009). The Conservatives: Trounced, Transfixed – And Transformed? In T. Casey (Ed.), *The Blair Legacy: Politics, Policy, Governance and Foreign Affairs* (pp. 52–64). Basingstoke: Palgrave.

Balogh, T. (1959). The Apotheosis of the Dilettente. In H. Thomas (Ed.), *Crisis in the Civil Service*. London: Blond.

Barry, F. (2009). Towards Improved Policy-Making in Ireland: Contestability and the Marketplace for Ideas. *Irish Journal of Public Policy, 3*(2), 1–12.

Beland, D., & Cox, R. H. (2011). *Ideas and Politics in Social Science Research*. Oxford: Oxford University Press.

© The Author(s) 2019
P. Diamond, *The End of Whitehall?*,
https://doi.org/10.1007/978-3-319-96101-9

Bentham, J. (2006). The IPPR and Demos: Think-Tanks of the New Social Democracy. *Political Quarterly, 77*(2), 166–176.

Bevir, M., & Rhodes, R. (2003). *Interpreting British Governance*. London: Routledge.

Blick, A. (2004). *People Who Live in the Dark: The History of the Special Adviser in British Politics*. London: Politico's.

Bouckaert, G. (2017). Taking Stock of 'Governance': A Predominantly European Perspective. *Governance, 30*(1), 45–52.

Bouckaert, G., & Mikeladze, M. (2008). Introduction. *NISPAee Journal of Public Administration, 1*(2), 7–8.

Bovaird, T., & Russell, K. (2007). Civil Service Reform in the UK 1999–2005: Revolutionary Failure or Evolutionary Success? *Public Administration, 85*(2), 301–328.

Brown, G. (2017). *My Life, Our Times*. London: Penguin Random House.

Bruce-Gardyne, J. (1986). *Inside the Whitehall Village: Ministers and Manadarins*. London: Sidgwick & Jackson.

Burnham, P. (2002). New Labour and the Politics of Depoliticisation. *British Journal of Politics and International Relations, 3*(2), 127–149.

Burnham, P., & Pyper, J. (2008). *Britain's Modernised Civil Service*. Basingstoke: Palgrave Macmillan.

Butler, D., et al. (1994). *Failure in British Government: The Politics of the Poll Tax*. Oxford: Oxford University Press.

Cairney, P. (2018). The UK Government's Imaginative Use of Evidence to Make Policy. *British Politics*, Forthcoming.

Campbell, C., & Wilson, G. (1995). *The End of Whitehall? Death of a Paradigm*. Oxford: Blackwells.

Cannadine, D. (2017). *Victorious Century: The United Kingdom 1800–1906*. London: Allen Lane.

Chapman, B. (1964). British Government Observed. *Public Administration, 42*(2), 184–185.

Christensen, J. (2014). *The Power of Economists Within the State*. Stanford: Stanford University Press.

Civil Service World. (2016, March 4). Margaret Hodge: Accountability System for Civil Servants Is 'Broken' – But MPs Are More Interested in New Policies Than Value for Money.

Clarke, J., & Newman, J. (1997). *The Managerial State*. London: Sage.

Clegg, N. (2016). *Politics: Between the Extremes*. London: Bodley Head.

Conservative Party. (2010). *General Election Manifesto 2010: An Invitation to the People of Britain*. London: The Conservative Party.

Craft, J. (2013). Appointed Political Staffs and the Diversification of Policy Advisory Sources: Theory and Evidence from Canada. *Policy and Society, 32*(3), 211–223.

Craft, J., & Halligan, J. (2015, July 1–4). *Looking Back and Thinking Ahead: 30 Years of Policy Advisory System Scholarship*. Prepared for T08P06 Comparing Policy Advisory Systems. International Conference on Public Policy. Catholic University of Sacro Cuore, Milan.

Craft, J., & Howlett, M. (2012). Policy Formulation, Governance Shifts and Policy Influence: Location and Content in Policy Advisory Systems. *Journal of Public Policy, 32*(2), 79–98.

Crewe, I., & King, A. (2013). *The Blunders of Our Governments*. London: One World Publications.

Crouch, C. (2011). *The Strange Non-Death of Neo-Liberalism*. Cambridge: Polity Press.

D'Ancona, M. (2014). *In It Together: The Inside Story of a Coalition Government*. London: Viking.

Davies, H. T. O., Nutley, S. M., & Smith, P. C. (2000). Introducing Evidence-Based Policy and Practice in Public Services. In H. T. O. Davies, S. M. Nutley, & P. C. Smith (Eds.), *What Works? Evidence-Based Policy and Practice in Public Services*. Bristol: Policy Press.

Denham, A., & Garnett, M. (2006). What Works? British Think-Tanks and the 'End of Ideology'. *Political Quarterly, 77*(2), 156–165.

Dommet, K., & Flinders, M. (2015). The Centre Strikes Back: Meta-Governance, Delegation, and the Core Executive in the United Kingdom 2010–2014. *Public Administration, 93*(1), 1–16.

Donnelly, M. (2014, June 30). Speech to the Institute of Government.

Downe, J., Andrews, R., & Guarneros-Meza, V. (2016). A Top-Down, Customer-Orientated Approach to Reform: Perceptions from UK Civil Servants. In G. Hammerschmid, S. Van de Walle, R. Andrews, & B. Bezes (Eds.), *Public Administration Reforms in Europe: The View from the Top*. Cheltenham: Edward Elgar Publishing.

Dudman, J. (2017, January 26). Brexit Won't Kill the Civil Service – But if You Use Public Services, Be Afraid. *The Guardian*.

Dunn, W. M., & Miller, D. Y. (2007). A Critique of the New Public Management and the Neo-Weberian State: Advancing a Critical Theory of Administrative Reform. *Public Organization Review, 7*(1), 345–358.

Eichbaum, C., & Shaw, R. (2007). Ministerial Advisers and the Politics of Policy-Making: Bureaucratic Permanence and Popular Control. *Australian Journal of Public Administration, 66*(4), 453–467.

Ferlie, L., Lynn, L., & Pollitt, C. (2010). In C. Moilanen & T. Demmke (Eds.), *Civil Services in the EU of 27*. Frankfurt: Peter Lang.

Fleischer, J. (2009). Power Resources of Parliamentary Executives: Policy Advice in the UK and Germany. *West European Politics, 32*(1), 196–214.

Flinders, M. (2010). The New British Constitution. *Political Studies Review, 8*(2), 262–263.

Foley, M. (1998). *The British Presidency*. Manchester: Manchester University Press.

Forsyth, J., & Nelson, F. (2016, December 10). Theresa May Interview: I Get so Frustrated with Whitehall. *The Spectator*.

Foster, C., & Plowden, W. (1998). *The State Under Stress*. Buckingham: Open University.

Fraussen, B., & Halpin, D. (2016). Think Tanks and Strategic Policymaking: The Contribution of Think Tanks to Policy Advisory Systems. *Policy Sciences, 50*(1), 105–124.

Freeguard, G., et al. (2015). *Whitehall Monitor 2015*. London: Institute for Government.

Freeguard, G., et al. (2017). *Whitehall Monitor 2017*. London: Institute for Government.

Gains, F., & Stoker, G. (2011). Special Advisers and the Transmission of Ideas from the Primeval Policy Soup. *Policy and Politics, 39*(4), 485–498(14).

Garner, R. (2011, September 23). Crisis of Confidence Among Civil Servants in Gove's Department. *The Independent*.

Gay, O., Schleiter, P., & Belu, V. (2015). The Coalition and the Decline of Majoritarianism in the UK. *Political Quarterly, 86*(1), 118–124.

Goes, E. (2015). *The Labour Party Under Ed Miliband*. Manchester: Manchester University Press.

Gouglas, A. (2016). *Paper Drafted for Internal Use in View of the Preparation for a KU Leuven OT Project on 'Policy Advice Utilisation in European Policy Advisory Systems'*. KU Leuven Public Management Institute.

Gouglas, A., & Brans, M. (2016, February 9). *UK Extended Ministerial Offices: On the Road to Cabinetisation?* London: Constitution Unit Blog. https://constitution-unit.com/2016/02/09/uk-extended-ministerial-offices-on-the-road-to-cabinetisation/

Grube, D. (2015). Responsibility to Be Enthusiastic? Public Servants and the Public Face of 'Promiscuous Partisanship'. *Governance, 28*(3), 305–320.

Grube, D., & Howard, C. (2016). Is the Westminster System Broken Beyond Repair? *Governance, 29*(4), 467–481.

Gunter, H. M., Hall, D., & Mills, C. (2015). Consultants, Consultancy and Consultocracy in Education Policymaking in England. *Journal of Education Policy, 30*(4), 518–539.

Guy-Peters, B. G., King, D., & Pierre, J. (2005). The Politics of Path Dependency: Political Conflict in Historical Institutionalism. *The Journal of Politics, 67*(4), 1275–1300.

Haddon, C. (2016). Developments in the Civil Service. In R. Heffernan, C. Hay, M. Russell, & P. Cowley (Eds.), *Developments in British Politics 10*. Basingstoke: Palgrave Macmillan.

Halligan, J. (1995). Policy Advice and the Public Sector. In B. G. Peters & D. T. Savoie (Eds.), *Governance in a Changing Environment* (pp. 138–172). Montreal: McGill-Queen's University Press.

Halligan, J. (2010). The Fate of Administrative Tradition in Anglophone Countries During the Reform Era. In M. Painter & B. G. Guy-Peters (Eds.), *Tradition and Public Administration*. Basingstoke: Palgrave Macmillan.

Hazell, R. (2012). How the Coalition Works at the Centre. In R. Hazell & B. Yong (Eds.), *The Politics of Coalition: How the Conservative-Liberal Democrat Government Works*. Oxford: Hart Publishing.

Hennessy, P. (1989). *Whitehall*. London: Fontana Press.

Hennessy, P. (1992). *Never Again: Britain 1945–51*. London: Jonathan Cape.

Hennessy, P. (1995). *The Hidden Wiring: Unearthing the British Constitution*. London: Weidenfeld & Nicholson.

Hennessy, P. (1998). *The Prime Minister: The Office and Its Holders*. Basingstoke: Palgrave Macmillan.

Hennessy, P. (2006). *Having It So Good: Britain in the 1950s*. London: Penguin.

Her Majesty's Government (HMG). (1968). *The Civil Service: Report of the Committee Chaired by Lord Fulton*. London: HMG.

Her Majesty's Government (HMG). (2012). *Civil Service Reform Plan*. London: HMG.

Hillman, N. (2016). The Coalition's Higher Education Reforms in England. *Oxford Review of Education, 42*(3), 330–345.

Hilton, S. (2015). *More Human: Designing a World Where People Come First*. London: Allen Lane.

Hood, C. (2001). *Public Service Bargains and Public Service Reform*. In B. G. Peters & J. Pierre (Eds.), *Politicians, Bureaucrats and Administrative Reform, Routledge/ECPR Studies in European Political Science* (pp. 13–23). London: Routledge.

Hood, C. (2007). What Happens When Transparency Meets Blame Avoidance. *Public Management Review, 9*(2), 191–210.

Horton, S. (2006). The Public Service Ethos in the British Civil Service: An Historical Institutionalist Perspective. *Public Policy and Administration, 21*(1), 32–48.

Hustedt, T., & Veit, S. (2017). Policy Advisory Systems: Change Dynamics and Sources of Variation. *Policy Sciences, 50*(1), 41–46.

Huxley, K., Andrews, R., Hammerschmid, G., & Van de Walle, S. (2016). Public Administration Reforms and Outcomes Across Countries and Policy Areas. In G. Hammerschmid, S. Van de Walle, R. Andrews, & B. Bezes (Eds.), *Public Administration Reforms in Europe: The View from the Top*. Cheltenham: Edward Elgar Publishing.

Independent Report of the Laidlaw Inquiry. (2012). *Inquiry into the Lessons Learned for the Department for Transport from the InterCity West Coast Competition*. HMG: Department of Transport.

Institute for Government (IfG). (2014). *Centre Forward: Effective Support for the Prime Minister at the Centre of Government*. London: IfG.

Institute for Government (IfG). (2018). *The Whitehall Monitor 2018: The General Election, Brexit and Beyond*. London: IfG.

Kerr, P., et al. (2011). Theorising Cameronism. *Political Studies Review, 9*(2), 56–71.

Kettl, D. (1997). The Revolution in Global Public Management: Driving Themes, Missing Links. *Journal of Policy Analysis and Management, 16*(3), 446–462.

Kidd, C. (2018, January 25). You Know Who You Are. *The London Review of Books.*

Kidd, C., & Rose, J. (2017). The Perils of Policy Advice. *Juncture, 23*(4), 242–253.

King, A., & Crewe, I. (2013). *The Blunders of Our Governments.* London: One World Publications.

Le Grand, J. (2006). *Of Knights and Knaves: Motivation, Agency and Public Policy.* Oxford: Oxford University Press.

Letwin, O. (2012, September 17). *Why Mandarins Matter: Keynote Speech.* London: Institute for Government.

Leys, C. (2006). The Cynical State. In *The Socialist Register.* London: Merlin Press.

Lijphart, A. (2012). *Patterns of Democracy.* New Haven: Yale University Press.

Lodge, G., & Pearce, N. (2012). *Accountability and Responsiveness in the Senior Civil Service: Lessons from Overseas.* London: IPPR.

Lowe, R. (2011). *The Official History of the British Civil Service: Reforming the Civil Service Volume I: The Fulton Years 1966–81.* London: Routledge.

Mackintosh, J. (1962). *The British Cabinet.* London: Stevens & Sons.

Macpherson, N. (2013, January 16). Speech by the Permanent Secretary to the Treasury, Sir Nicholas Macpherson: The Origins of Treasury Control. https://www.gov.uk/government/speeches/speech-by-the-permanent-secretary-to-the-treasury-sir-nicholas-macpherson-the-origins-of-treasury-control

Marquand, D. (1988). *The Unprincipled Society.* London: Jonathan Cape.

Marquand, D. (2008). *Britain Since 1918: The Strange Career of British Democracy.* London: Weidenfeld & Nicholson.

Marquand, D. (2014). *Mammon's Kingdom: An Essay on Britain, Now.* London: Allen Lane.

Matthews, F. (2012). The Capacity to Co-ordinate: Whitehall, Governance and the Challenge of Climate Change. *Public Policy & Administration, 27*(2), 169–189.

Matthews, F., & Flinders, M. (2016). Patterns of Democracy: Coalition Government and Majoritarian Modification in the UK 2010–15. *British Politics,* Early View Online.

McClory, J. (2010, November 10). *Will 'New Style' Departmental Boards Kill or Cure?* London: Institute for Government.

Moran, M. (2003). *The Regulatory State.* Oxford: Oxford University Press.

Morgan, G., & Sturdy, A. (2017). The Role of Large Management Consultancy Firms in Global Public Policy. In D. Stone & K. Maloney (Eds.), *Oxford Handbook on Global Public Policy and Transnational Administration.* Oxford: Oxford University Press.

Muir, R. (1930). *How Britain Is Governed: A Critical Analysis of Modern Developments in the British System of Government.* London: Constable & Company Ltd.

Mulgan, G. (2006). Thinking in Tanks: The Changing Ecology of Political Ideas. *Political Quarterly, 77*(2), 147–155.

Mulgan, R. (2007). Truth in Government and the Politicisation of Public Service Advice. *Public Administration, 85*(3), 569–586.

Niskanen, W. A. (1971). *Bureaucracy and Representative Government.* Chicago: Aldine-Atherton.

Niskanen, W. A. (1994). *Bureaucracy and Public Economics.* Vermont: Edward Elgar Publishing.

Norman, J., & Ganesh, J. (2006). *Compassionate Conservatism: What It Is and Why We Need It.* London: Policy Exchange.

Normington, D. (2013, January 16). Letter to the Times Newspaper.

Norris, E., Kidson, M., Bouchal, P., & Rutter, J. (2014). *Doing Them Justice: Lessons from Four Cases of Policy Implementation.* London: Institute for Government/Joseph Rowntree Foundation.

O'Malley, M. (2017). Temporary Partisans, Tagged Officers or Impartial Professionals: Moving Between Ministerial Offices and Departments. *Public Administration, 95*(1), 407–420.

Page, E. (2010). Has the Whitehall Model Survived? *International Journal of Administrative Sciences, 76*(3), 407–423.

Parker, G. (2016, April 13). Veteran of Treasury Battles Tots up a Decade's Wins and Losses. *The Financial Times.*

Paun, A., & Harris, J. (2012). *Reforming Civil Service Accountability.* London: Institute for Government.

Paun, A., & Harris, J. (2013). *Accountability at the Top: Supporting Effective Leadership in Whitehall.* London: Institute for Government.

Paun, A., et al. (2010). *Shaping Up: A Whitehall for the Future?* London: Institute for Government.

Pedersen, A., Sehested, K., & Sorenson, E. (2011). Emerging Theoretical Understanding of Pluricentric Coordination in Public Governance. *The American Review of Public Administration, 41*(1), 372–395.

Peters, B. G. (2000). *The Future of Governing* (2nd ed.). Lawrence: University Press of Kansas.

Peters, B. G. (2005). The Problem of Policy Problems. *Journal of Comparative Policy Analysis: Research and Practice, 7*(4), 349–370.

Peters, G., & Pierre, J. (2004). *Politicisation of the Civil Service in Comparative Perspective: The Quest for Control.* London: Routledge.

Peters, G.-P., & Savoie, D. (1994). Civil Service Reform: Misdiagnosing the Patient. *Public Administration Review, 54*(5), 418–425.

Peters, G.-P., & Savoie, D. (2012). In Search of Good Governance. In H. Bakvis & M. Jarvis (Eds.), *From New Public Management to New Political Governance* (pp. 29–45). McGill-Queens University Press.

Pierson, P. (2004). *Politics in Time*. Princeton: Princeton University Press.

Pierson, P., & Skocpol, T. (2002). Historical Institutionalism in Contemporary Political Science. In I. Katznelson & H. Milner (Eds.), *Political Science: The State of the Discipline* (pp. 445–488). New York: Norton.

Pollit, C. (2010). Cuts and Reforms – Public Services as We Move into a New Era. *Society and Economy, 32*(1), 17–31.

Qvortrup, M. (2005). *Memorandum to the Select Committee on Public Administration – Written Evidence*. London: House of Commons.

Rhodes, R. A. W. (1994). The Hollowing Out of the State: The Changing Nature of the Public Service in Britain. *The Political Quarterly, 65*(2), 138–151.

Rhodes, R. A. W. (1997). *Understanding Governance: Policy Networks, Governance, Reflexivity and Accountability*. Philadelphia, PA: Open University Press.

Rhodes, R. A. W. (2011a). *Everyday Life in British Government*. Oxford: Oxford University Press.

Rhodes, R. A. W. (2011b). One-Way, Two-Way, or Dead-End Street: The British Influence on American Public Administration. *Public Administration Review, 74*(4), 559–571.

Richards, S. (2010). *Whatever It Takes: The Real Story of Gordon Brown and New Labour*. London: Fourth Estate.

Richards, D., & Smith, M. (2016). The Westminster Model and the 'Indivisibility of the Political and Economic Elite': A Convenient Myth Whose Time Is up? *Governance, 29*(4), 499–516.

Richardson, J. (2017). The Changing British Policy Style: From Governance to Government? *British Politics*, Forthcoming.

Runciman, D. (2014). *Politics: Ideas in Profile*. London: Profile Books.

Rutter, J. (2013, June 19). Ministers Should Commission IPPR and Civil Service Advice in Parallel. *The Guardian*.

Saint-Martin, D. (1998). Les consultants et la réforme managérialiste de l'État en France et en Grande-Bretagne: vers l'émergence d'une 'consultocratie'? *Revue canadienne de science politique, 32*(1), 41–74.

Sausman, C., & Locke, R. (2004). The British Civil Service: Examining the Question of Politicisation. In G. B. Peters & J. Pierre (Eds.), *Politicisation of the Civil Service in Comparative Perspective* (pp. 101–124). London: Routledge.

Savoie, D. (2008). *Court Government and the Collapse of Accountability in Canada and the United Kingdom*. Toronto: University of Toronto Press.

Savoie, D. (2010). *Court Government and the Collapse of Accountability in the UK and Canada*. Toronto: Toronto University Press.

Seldon, A. (2017). *Blair Unbound*. London: Weidenfeld & Nicholson.

Shaw, S. E., Russell, J., Parsons, W., & Greenhalgh, T. (2015). The View from Nowhere? How Think-Tanks Work to Shape Health Policy. *Critical Policy Studies, 9*(1), 58–77.

Shipman, T. (2017). *Fall Out: A Year of Political Mayhem*. London: William Collins.

Skelcher, C. (2000). Changing Images of the State: Overloaded, Hollowed-Out, Congested. *Public Policy & Administration, 15*(3), 3–19.

Skidelsky, R. (2013). *Keynes: Economist, Philosopher, Statesman.* London: Penguin.

Smith, M. J., & Jones, R. (2015). From Big Society to Small State: Conservatism and the Privatisation of Government. *British Politics, 10*(2), 226–248.

Stone, D. (2006). Think-Tanks and Policy Analysis. In F. Fischer, G. J. Miller, & M. S. Sidney (Eds.), *Handbook of Public Policy Analysis: Theory, Methods and Politics* (pp. 149–157). New York: Marcel Dekker Inc.

Straw, E. (2004). *The Dead Generalist: Reforming the Civil Service and Public Services.* London: Demos.

Theakston, K. (2015). David Cameron as Prime Minister. *British Politics Review, 10*(2), 6–7.

Thelen, K. (1999). Historical Institutionalism in Comparative Politics. *Annual Review of Political Science, 2*, 369–404.

Thelen, K., & Steinmo, S. (1992). Historical Institutionalism in Comparative Politics. In S. Steinmo, K. Thelen, & F. Longstreth (Eds.), *Structuring Politics: Historical Institutionalism in Comparative Analysis.* Cambridge: Cambridge University Press.

Van de Walle, S., & Hammerschmid, G. (2011). The Impact of the New Public Management: Challenges for Coordination and Cohesion in European Public Sectors. *Administrative Culture, 12*(2), 190–202.

Van den Berg, C. (2016). Dynamics in the Dutch Policy Advisory System: Externalisation, Politicisation and the Legacy of Pillarisation. *Policy Sciences, 50*(1), 63–84.

Van der Meer, F. M., Raadschelders, J., & Toonen, M. (2015). Introduction. In F. M. Van der Meer, J. Raadschelders, & M. Toonen (Eds.), *Civil Service Systems in the 21st Century.* Basingstoke: Palgrave Macmillan.

Vesely, A. (2016). Policy Advice as Policy Work: A Conceptual Framework for Multi-Level Analysis. *Policy Sciences, 50*(1), 1–14.

Waller, P. (2012). Departments: Ministers and the Civil Service. In R. Hazell & B. Yong (Eds.), *The Politics of Coalition: How the Conservative-Liberal Democrat Government Works.* Oxford: Hart Publishing.

Watts, R. (2013, February 16). Ministers' New Plan to Steamroller Civil Servants. *The Daily Telegraph.*

Weber, M. (2014). Politics as a Vocation: Originally a Speech at Munich University 1918. In T. Waters & D. Waters (Eds.), *Weber's Rationalism and Modern Society.* New York: Palgrave Macmillan.

Weber, M. (2015). *Weber's Rationalism and Modern Society.* Basingstoke: Palgrave Macmillan.

Wildavsky, A. (1979). *Speaking Truth to Power: The Art and Craft of Policy Analysis.* New York: Little Brown.

Yong, B., & Hazell, R. (2014). *Special Advisers: What They Do and Why They Matter.* London: Bloomsbury.

Index[1]

A

Anglophone countries, 44, 58, 87
Anti-politics, 49, 88
Attlee, Clement, 2, 4n8, 64, 87
Aucoin, Peter, 1, 2, 2n3, 9, 10, 13, 16, 23, 46, 58, 59, 65, 71, 72, 78, 80, 82, 85
Austerity, 16, 40, 71, 72, 75, 80, 84
Australia, 2n3, 37, 45, 59, 68

B

Benn, Tony, 7
Better Government Initiative, 36, 59
Beveridge, William, 4
Blair, Tony, 1, 8–10, 8n16, 24–26, 33, 35, 60, 79, 87, 89
Blame games, 73
Brexit, 73, 90
Brown, Gordon, 9, 35
Bureaucracy, 1–7, 1n2, 10, 13–17, 26–28, 31, 33, 37, 39, 41, 42, 44, 48, 51, 52, 60, 61, 63, 64, 71–78, 80, 83, 85–87, 89, 90

Bureaucrats, 2–4, 7, 14, 33, 38, 39, 42, 47, 51, 58, 78, 80, 84, 86
Butler, Robin, 50

C

Cabinet, 8, 8n16, 9, 23–26
Cabinet government, 9, 10, 24
Cabinet Office, 10, 26, 27, 32, 35, 45, 46n50, 50, 68
Cabinet Secretary, 2, 4, 7, 8, 11, 16n29, 37, 44, 50, 51, 61, 62, 67
Cameron, David, 2, 10–11, 13, 17, 24–28, 35, 39, 44, 50–52, 58, 60–63, 73, 75, 79, 80
Campbell, Colin, 3, 4, 16
Canada, 2n3
Cannadine, David, 57, 58, 77
Chief executives, 24, 27, 59, 65, 73
Civil service, 1–4, 1n2, 6–9, 11–13, 16, 17, 23, 24, 26, 27, 31–47, 49, 50, 52, 57, 58, 60–61, 63–69, 71–79, 81–83, 85, 88–90
Civil Service Reform Plan, 15, 36

[1] Note: Page numbers followed by 'n' refer to notes.

© The Author(s) 2019
P. Diamond, *The End of Whitehall?*,
https://doi.org/10.1007/978-3-319-96101-9

Clegg, Nick, 11, 26, 41
Club government, 4
Coalition government, 10, 34
Competition, 14, 44, 60, 62, 64
Conservative Party manifesto, 12
Consultocracy, 48
Consumer model of political choice, 15
Contestable policy fund, 45–48
Court government, 13, 14
Cuts, public sector budget, 81

D
Departmental secretaries, 11, 59
Department of Communities and Local
    Government (DCLG), 51, 81
Department of Work and Pensions
    (DWP), 17, 43, 82
Director-Generals, 32, 61, 63, 67, 84

E
Economic and Domestic Secretariat
    (EDS), 26
Efficiency, 2, 7, 24, 50, 79
European Union (EU), 16, 73, 88, 90
Evidence-based policy, 15, 50, 86
Extended Ministerial Offices (EMOs),
    27, 36–37, 46, 60

F
Freedom of Information, 38
Fulton Report, 9, 41, 42

G
Gove, Michael, 33, 40, 66, 67
Governance, 2–3, 11, 13–16, 24–26,
    31, 57, 58, 61, 66, 68, 78,
    83–85, 88, 89
Government Information Service
    (GIS), 26

H
Haldane report, 3
Halligan, John, 5, 44, 47, 71, 82
Hennessy, Peter, 4, 6, 8, 9, 34, 36, 60
Heywood, Jeremy, 11, 26, 50, 51, 68
Hilton, Steve, 11, 27, 39, 79
Historical institutionalism, 5, 6, 16,
    82
Hollowing-out, 14, 84, 88
Hunt, John, 7
Hyper-innovation, 3, 7, 8, 12

I
Ideal-type bureaucracy, 4, 52
Ideas, role of, 82, 87
Institute for Government (IfG), 25,
    46, 47, 50, 61, 62, 69, 73, 85

K
Kerslake, Bob, 51, 67
Keynes, John Maynard, 4, 5

L
Laidlaw report, 84
Laws, David, 40
Letwin, Oliver, 42, 50, 84
Leys, Colin, 6, 15, 47, 48, 80
Loyalty paradox, 4, 72

M
Machiavelli, Niccolo, 17
Macpherson, Nicholas, 61, 73–75
Management consultancy, 37, 46–48,
    51
Managerial politicisation, 34, 35
Managers, 6, 9, 14, 15, 64, 65, 77,
    83, 84
Marketization, 48
Market state, 77, 87

Maude, Francis, 11, 13–15, 39, 41, 42, 45, 46, 62, 65, 67, 68, 72, 79, 84
May, Theresa, 2, 17, 28, 61, 67, 68, 85
Monopoly, over policy-making, 44, 47, 71

N
Neo-liberalism, 86
Neo-Weberian, 89
New media, 88
New Political Governance (NPG), 1–3, 10–11, 13–16, 18, 23, 26, 58, 59, 68, 71, 77–80, 82, 86–90
New Public Management (NPM), 12–15, 58, 86, 87, 89
New Zealand, 2n3, 10, 59, 62
Next Steps agencies, 84
Non-governmental organisations (NGOs), 36, 47
Normington, David, 42, 61, 63
Northcote-Trevelyan report, 3, 36, 45, 57, 58, 60, 63, 77, 85, 89
Number Ten Downing Street, 24, 25
Number Ten Press Office, 25

O
Osborne, George, 24, 26, 27, 75, 81

P
Permanent campaign, 9, 15, 16, 23–28, 33, 34, 52, 59, 75, 77, 87–89
Personalisation of appointments, 16, 57–69
Platonic ideal, 27, 88
Policy advisory system, 44
Policy-based evidence (PBE), 43

Policy blunders, 3, 24, 88
Policy delivery, 84
Policy entrepreneurs, 33, 44, 46
Policy fiascos, 6, 89
Policy implementation, 72
Policy-making process, 13, 14, 18, 45, 51, 76, 87
Policy-related politicisation, 36
Political parties, 6, 23, 48, 49, 77, 87
Political patronage, 57, 58, 65
Politicisation, 2, 31, 32, 34, 48, 58, 61, 62, 72, 78, 86, 88
Politics as a Vocation, 23
Poll Tax, 25
Post-bureaucratic state (PBS), 6, 11–13, 15, 18
Post-truth democracy, 49
Prime Minister, 2, 4, 7, 9–13, 17, 23–27, 32, 32n1, 35, 36, 46, 50, 51, 59, 61, 62, 66, 68, 79, 80, 85
Prime ministerial government, 11, 13, 44, 63, 75, 79
Prime Minister's Delivery Unit (PMDU), 35
Prime Minister's Office, 11, 13, 23
Prime Minister's Policy Unit, 25, 27, 35
Prime Minister's Strategy Unit, 38n23, 42n39, 79n5
Principal-agent theory, 14
Private sector, 9, 11–14, 64, 65, 83, 86, 88
Promiscuous partisanship, 71, 72, 75, 78
Public administration, 2–5, 10, 13, 15, 16, 23, 77, 78, 89
Public Administration Select Committee (PASC), 36, 63, 84
Public sector, 7, 11, 12, 16, 48, 49, 64, 65, 78, 81, 82, 84
Public services, 3, 7, 9–11, 31, 34, 77, 78, 85–89
Purdah guidelines, 73

Q

Quasi-markets, 9, 14, 82

R

Reagan, Ronald, 7, 87
Recruitment, 12, 64, 65, 87

S

Savoie, Donald, 4, 6, 7, 9, 13–15, 17,
    25, 26, 28, 35, 59, 65, 68, 85
Scotland, 1n2, 73, 74, 90
Scottish independence referendum, 73
Secretary of State, 28, 34, 60–62,
    65–67
Skidelsky, Robert, 5
Sofa government, 8, 8n16, 13, 25, 85
Special advisers, 7, 8, 16n29, 25,
    31–37, 40, 45, 48, 49, 51, 59
Special Advisers' Code, 35
Street-level bureaucrats, 7, 39, 84

T

Thatcher, Margaret, 1, 7–9, 23, 64
The Thick of It, 31

Think-tanks, 12, 15, 37, 38, 45–49,
    51, 87, 90
Trade unions, 48
Treasury, 12, 61, 67, 68, 72–75,
    83
Turnbull, Andrew, 50

U

UK Statistics Authority, 28

W

Weber, Max, 3, 4, 14, 15, 23, 28, 32,
    52, 85, 86
Westminster model, 10, 11
What works, 50, 86
Whitehall model, 1, 3–6, 10, 16, 31,
    34, 36, 47, 49, 57, 59, 68, 69,
    78, 80, 83, 86, 88
Whitehall village, 4, 6
Wicked problems, 89, 89n20
Wilson, Graham, 3, 4, 16

Y

Yes, Minister, 31

Printed in the United States
By Bookmasters